BASKETBALL MADE SIMPLE: A SPECTATOR'S GUIDE

by P.J. Harari and Dave Ominsky

Illustrated by Stephen J. Lattimer
Cover design by Eugene Cheltenham
Hand signals by Anna Mendoza

Photographs © by
Allsport Photography and Bruce Bennett Studios

©1994 First Base Sports, Inc., Los Angeles, California

Look for these other Spectator Guides:
- Baseball Made Simple
- Football Made Simple
- Ice Hockey Made Simple
- Olympics Made Simple
- Soccer Made Simple

ISBN 1-884309-03-8
Library of Congress Catalog Card Number: 94-96357

We welcome your comments and questions:
FIRST BASE SPORTS, INC.
P.O. BOX 1731
MANHATTAN BEACH, CALIFORNIA 90267-1731
(310) 318-3006

Typesetting by Jelico Computing

HOW TO USE THIS BOOK

Basketball is played more than any other American team sport —in 99% of U.S. high schools and colleges, and in over 130 countries — with avid spectators worldwide. Fans gaze in wonder at the grace and physical strength of these players whether they be children on city playgrounds, adults in gymnasiums, student athletes at colleges or the *Dream Team* at the Olympics. Basketball seems a simple game, yet understanding its rich subtleties is not easy.

This book aims to educate anyone who wants to know more about this exciting international game. It is written for use by a variety of audiences — adults who want to become fans, children who want to learn the basics of the sport they are playing and even existing fans who want a quick reference guide to their favorite sport.

Each chapter has been written to stand alone, so you do not have to sit and read the book from cover to cover. However, the chapters do build on each other, so if you start at page 1 and read through to the end, the chapters flow logically and become more detailed as you progress.

This book will mainly discuss the rules of basketball as played at the professional level in the United States. However, this book will also outline the differences in the rules used at the college level where they are important.

Rules, as well as any word or phrase printed in *italics*, can be referenced quickly and easily using the book's glossary or index. So get ready to learn about basketball — the most popular American sport.

ORGANIZATIONS IN BASKETBALL

Federation Internationale de Basketball Association (FIBA): The governing body of international basketball was founded in 1932 and today has 195 member nations. Every 4 years it stages a 16-nation *World Cup* of Basketball, the most recent of which was in Toronto in August 1994 (won by U.S.'s *Dream Team II*).

National Basketball Association (NBA): The most popular professional league in the world today was created by the merger of the *Basketball Association of America* and the *National Basketball League* in 1949. It currently has 27 teams in the U.S., and by 1995 will add 2 more in Canada. Its stars have worldwide appeal and over 117 nations watch its championships on TV. The NBA's headquarters are in New York.

National College Athletic Association (NCAA): This voluntary association of U.S. colleges establishes rules and standards for their athletics. It first developed rules for basketball in 1908. Since 1939 it has hosted a tournament of the best college teams in the U.S. that culminates in the *Final Four* and crowns an annual college champion. Though it started with only 8 teams, the field for this tournament has grown to 64 teams today. Its headquarters are in Overland, Kansas.

Continental Basketball Association (CBA): This developmental league for the NBA, started in 1979, has 16 professional teams. From November through March it plays a 56-game season, culminating with *playoffs* in April. To ensure stability, the CBA now requires its 10-man *rosters* to have at least 1 *rookie* and 2 other players with less than 3 years of professional experience. It is headquartered in St. Louis, Missouri.

Foreign leagues: Approximately 300 Americans are playing abroad on every continent, although the most competitive leagues are in Europe. Players are enticed with larger monetary contracts than they can get at home as the international market grows saturated with over-the-hill NBA and CBA players.

TABLE OF CONTENTS

ORIGINS & HISTORY OF BASKETBALL

Basketball is the only competitive team sport that completely originated in the United States. It started in Springfield, Massachusetts in December 1891 when a young Canadian, *James A. Naismith* (See **Fig. 1**), while studying for the Presbyterian ministry, enrolled at the YMCA Training School because he wanted to do more than preach. The students there, who were studying to be YMCA athletic directors and secretaries, so disliked calisthenics that the head of the athletic department asked Dr. Naismith to devise an indoor game to replace these and fill the void between the football and baseball seasons.

Dr. Naismith's original basketball game employed 2 wooden peach baskets nailed to the boards of the gymnasium, 13 rules (5 of which still govern the game

Fig. 1: Dr. Naismith holding his peach basket.

today) and 9 members on each team (simply because he had 18 students in his class). He was inspired by football, rugby, soccer, water polo, field hockey and lacrosse in creating his new sport although his rules stressed less contact than some of these sports. By placing the basket high up, he hoped to create a game of skill rather than power and size. (In fact, as the rules evolved over the years, many attempts were made to curb the advantages of height — but each time players adapted by increasing their range of skills.) When players grew tired of climbing with a ladder to reclaim the ball after every goal, the bottom of the basket was removed.

The game became an instant success as people across the country requested copies of the rules. Within 3 years it was introduced in Canada, Europe and as far as Australia, China and India — and the rules were printed in 30 languages. During those early years the game was often rough and dangerous. To protect the spectators from players chasing the ball into the stands, a wire cage was built around the court — which is the reason basketball is still sometimes referred to as the cage game. The players would get cut from being thrown against the wires and the court was often covered with blood. Teams used only *layups* and 2-handed *set shots* to score before crowds of raucous fans.

That success did not last long, however. By the turn of the century, basketball fell into disrepute as it became even rougher. Also, gymnasiums that could otherwise be used by as many as 60 people at a time doing a variety of things were increasingly tied up with basketball games of only 18 players, limiting the gym's availability to the general public.

This situation actually spurred the start of the professional game in the U.S. Players were forced to rent dance halls, skating rinks and other spacious locations to accommodate their game. They began charging admission to cover the rental fees and split any profits. Games at these unusual sites were often played around obstacles, such as pillars or posts. Opponents could be forced into these for a "post" play — a term still used to describe when a player acts as a pillar (or *screen*) for a teammate in the *post*.

But these early leagues lacked stability and were often short-lived. The most well-known team in the 1920s was the *Original Celtics* who traveled from city to city beating the best teams. When the professional *American Basketball League* (*ABL*) was formed with 9 teams in 1925, the Celtics reluctantly joined and fans grew bored as the Celtics won nearly every game. The first all-black team, the *Rens* (formed because they were not permitted to join the early leagues), came on the scene around the same time and a few years later a team of black basketball entertainers, the *Harlem Globetrotters*, also began touring the country. These are discussed in the chapter on **GREAT TEAMS & DYNASTIES**.

Outside the U.S., basketball's popularity did not truly blossom until the late 1930s, when the sport was added to the 1936 Olympic Games and as U.S. servicemen stationed on foreign soil provided instruction abroad. Meanwhile, in the U.S., the leagues were in a state of disarray by 1930, following the economic setback of the Depression and waning interest. Basketball was kept alive at home by the more than 50 colleges that continued to play the game.

The sport's biggest strides came during the next 10 years due to 5 main factors: the building of large arenas, the introduction of big-time college basketball at Madison Square Garden (which brought about the creation of standardized rules and officiating), the introduction of a high-scoring version of the game, the acceptance of the one-handed shot and annual tournaments (such as the *NIT*'s introduced in 1938 and the *NCAA*'s in 1939) which provided a goal for the country's best college teams.

The success of the college game encouraged the founding of the professional *National Basketball League* (*NBL*) in 1937 with 13 teams and the corporate sponsor support of Goodyear, Firestone and General Electric. However, the advent of World War II halted the new league's progress. It was not until 1946 that Walter A. Brown, president of Boston Garden, organized the first truly ordered professional league, the *Basketball Association of America* (*BAA*). In 1949 it merged with the remains of the NBL to form the *National Basketball Association* (*NBA*) which still exists today. A rival league, the *American Basketball Association* (*ABA*) was founded in 1967, but folded in 1976, merging some of its teams into the NBA.

It was in the 1970s that basketball's popularity exploded. By 1977, over 100 million spectators were attending organized basketball games at the high school, college and professional levels in the U.S. each year. The frequency of televised college games spurred on this growing interest. Today, the NCAA's *Final Four* tournament is one of the nation's major sporting events, rivaling the Super Bowl and World Series in number of viewers — over 50 million watched the 1993 final game.

Women were involved with basketball from the start. It was first played by the teachers at the Buckingham School in Springfield (including Maude Sherman, who would become Dr. Naismith's wife), but it was truly pioneered by Smith College who introduced the game in 1892. The first rules for women were encoded by Clara Baer of Newcomb College (New Orleans) in 1895.

What started as a slow, non-contact sport in Dr. Naismith's mind has evolved into a modern-day game of speed, grace, power and tremendous skill. Let us next turn to the **OBJECT OF THE GAME** as we begin our journey to understanding this popular American sport.

OBJECT OF BASKETBALL

Basketball is a fast-
paced game played
by 2 teams of 5 players
each. The object is to toss
a *ball* into the opposing
team's *basket* to score *points*
while preventing that team from
doing the same. The team that scores
the most points is the winner.

Although the game is usually played indoors, it can also be
played on outdoor playgrounds, in garage driveways or
anywhere else a basket can be set up. The fact that it can
be played inside or out creates a year-round sport. Also,
since the game requires no other equipment besides a ball
and a basket, its easy set-up makes it equally popular
among players of all ages in cities, suburbs and
countrysides around the world.

Basketball's rules are continually evolving with an eye
toward preserving a game of skill rather than brute force,
in keeping with the original intentions of its creator, *Dr.
Naismith*. These rules are also designed to keep the game
moving while protecting players from injury — no small
feat when so many large players vie for control of a ball in
a rather small area.

Basketball may seem to be such a simple game, yet there
are important rules and strategies you can learn that will
make it more fun to watch. With this notion in mind and
the help of this book — which covers the rules and
strategies of the professional and college game in the
U.S.— you should be able to understand nuances of
basketball you never noticed before, and enjoy it that much
more.

THE BASKETBALL COURT

An indoor regulation-sized basketball *court* has a hardwood surface and is rectangular in shape. Its maximum dimensions are 94 x 50 feet and there is no rule that specifies how small a court may be. It is common today for arenas to have the home team's logo painted onto the hardwood surface.

The court's boundaries are called *sidelines* along its length and *end lines* (or *baselines*) along its width. (See **Fig. 2**) When a player with the ball (or the ball itself) touches any part of these lines or the area outside of them, he is considered *out of bounds* and his team loses *possession* of the ball. (See **Fig. 3**) However, a player can make an acrobatic play that saves a ball from going out of bounds and the action continues even if that player lands out of bounds.

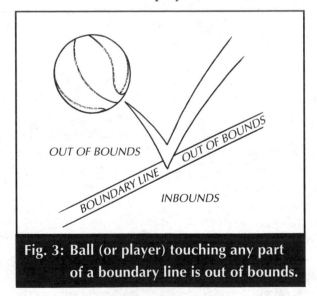

OUT OF BOUNDS

OUT OF BOUNDS

BOUNDARY LINE

INBOUNDS

Fig. 3: Ball (or player) touching any part of a boundary line is out of bounds.

Basket, Rim and Backboard

At each end of the court a *basket* is attached to the lower center of a *backboard* generally made of transparent plexiglass (See **Fig. 4**). Each basket consists of a horizontal

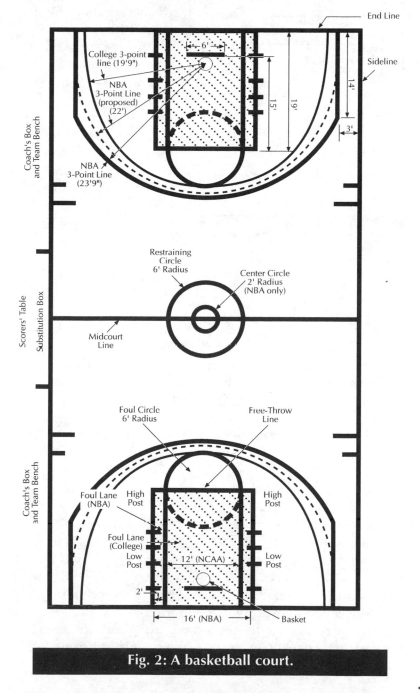

Fig. 2: A basketball court.

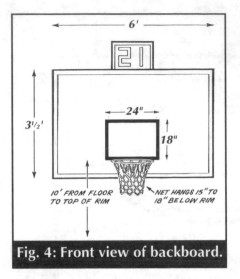

Fig. 4: Front view of backboard.

metal ring 18" in diameter called the *rim* placed 10 feet above the court's surface with a bottomless *net* 15"-18" in length hanging from it. A small white rectangle is painted on the backboard above the rim to provide a target area for shooting the ball. A *shot clock* with big red numbers is also visible above each basket. In college, it is sometimes located on the floor just outside the corner of the court. A red electric light is also placed behind the backboard to signal the end of each *period*.

Each backboard is suspended 4 feet inside the end line, by a base located out of bounds. (See **Fig. 5**) This allows players room to maneuver behind the basket without going out of bounds. The base is padded to protect players who might accidentally collide with it. Some college arenas have backboards suspended from the ceiling for easier maintenance and to offer fans an unobstructed view of the game.

An interesting sidenote on backboards: they were once made of wood and metal (still used in high schools and gymnasiums), but were changed to glass to allow spectators to see through them. Today, plexiglass is used because it does not shatter as easily during play, and if it does, its falling pieces are less dangerous. While this used to be a rare occurrence, the advent of bigger and more athletic players is making this a more common problem. In fact, the *NBA* recently started requiring each arena to have an extra backboard unit on the premises during games to prevent costly delays if a backboard shatters.

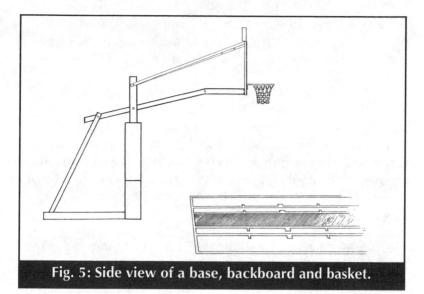

Fig. 5: Side view of a base, backboard and basket.

<u>Lines on the Court</u>

Dividing the Court — The *center* or *midcourt line* runs parallel to the end lines and divides the court into two halves called the *frontcourt* and the *backcourt*. The frontcourt contains the basket at which Team A is shooting to score points; the backcourt is the area Team A is defending (where Team A is trying to stop Team B from scoring). Only the team on offense has a frontcourt and backcourt. When Team B becomes the offense, its frontcourt is where Team A's backcourt used to be.

In addition to the midcourt line, several other important lines are painted on the court's surface:

Center Circle — At the center of the court are 2 circles which are used for *jump balls* including the one that starts the game. One is 2 feet in diameter (the *jumping circle* — NBA only) surrounded by another 12 feet in diameter (the *restraining circle*), and together they are called the center circle. Two other 12-foot *foul circles*, located one at each end of the court, are also used for jump balls.

Foul Line (or *Free-Throw Line*) — a line 16' long (12' in college) located 15' away from the backboard from which players take unobstructed shots at the basket (called *free-throws* or *foul shots*) after a *foul* is committed by the opposing team.

Foul Lane — an area 19' long and 16' wide (12' in college), bordered by the end line and the foul line. Players must stand with both feet outside this lane area during a free-throw. The entire foul lane is painted a different color than the rest of the court. A player standing in it is said to be *in the paint*. The NBA is considering enlarging the foul lane this coming season.

The *Key* — At each end of the court is a key (named for the keyhole shape this area had many years ago). The 3 elements of the key are the foul circle, the foul lane and the free-throw line.

3-Point Line — In each half of the court is drawn a large horseshoe-shaped line called the 3-point line. In the NBA, this line is approximately 23'9" from the basket though it may be changed to 22' as soon as next season (it is 19'9" in college, with a slightly different shape). Players who shoot the ball into the basket while standing with both feet completely behind this line (or one foot, if the other is in mid-air) earn 3 points — the maximum for any single shot.

Areas Located Out of Bounds — Various hash marks are also drawn along the sidelines. These designate, among other things, the 8 foot *substitution box* in front of the *scorers' table* where players wait to enter the game, and the *coaches' boxes*, the area beyond which the coaches cannot roam during play. Along the same side of the court are 2 benches (or chairs) where the players, coaches and trainers from each team sit during the game. Separating these 2 benches is the scorers' table, where the *scorers* and *timekeepers* sit.

Now let us see what **UNIFORMS & EQUIPMENT** players use.

UNIFORMS & EQUIPMENT

Much of basketball's popularity can be attributed to its simple needs in player and *court* equipment. It is easy for any player with a pair of athletic shoes to find a simple *rim* attached to a wall or pole to practice *shooting*. All he needs is one other friend to play a game of *one-on-one*. Basketball is an inexpensive sport whose set-up is readily available everywhere in the world.

Professional basketball players wear simple *uniforms* — shorts and sleeveless jerseys adorned with their team's logo. During games, the home team wears light-colored uniforms and visitors wear darker-colored ones. A player's number is printed 6" high on both sides of the jersey, and his name appears on the back. Today, players often wear a short-sleeved T-shirt underneath their jersey, and the shorts seem to get longer every season. A few players even wear 2 pairs of shorts, with a longer pair beneath the official trunks — a style readily mimicked by American kids.

The basketball shoes worn by players are sneakers called high-tops, designed to support and protect the ankles. New designs with innovative features are continually introduced by the biggest athletic shoe companies, such as shoes with air pumps. These are highly coveted by youngsters who try to emulate the star athletes. One famous television ad claimed (tongue-in-cheek) "it was the shoes" that gave *Michael Jordan* his incredible leaping ability.

The equipment is also simple — a *ball* and a *basket*. The ball itself is an inflated sphere made of an airtight rubber casing covered with leather that is about 30 inches in circumference and weighs about 22 ounces. It is inflated to 7 ½ or 8 ½ pounds of pressure.

Now let us see how points are scored using this ball as we turn to the chapter on **SCORING**.

SCORING

There are 2 ways to score in basketball: a *field goal* or a *free-throw*. A field goal is scored anytime the ball comes down through the top of the *basket* during play. It counts for 2 *points*, unless it is thrown by a player with both feet on the *floor* completely behind the *3-point line* (or at least one foot if the other is in mid-air), where it counts as a *3-point shot*. *Inside shooting* occurs near the basket, usually in the *key*, while *outside (perimeter) shooting* occurs from beyond the *foul line*.

A free-throw is a shot taken from the foul line by a player who is un*guard*ed. Each successful free-throw counts for 1 point. One or 2 free-throws are taken when a player *goes to the line* depending on the situation that brought him there (i.e., whether the opponent committed a *personal* or *technical foul*, discussed in the chapter on **VIOLATIONS & FOULS**). In college (and the *NBA* is considering changing its rules too), players who are fouled in the process of shooting a 3-point shot get 3 free-throws.

Free-throws are generally easier to make because the shooter is not distracted by any opponents and he can take up to 10 seconds in preparing his shot. Between 20-30% of the points in an *NBA* game come from free-throws, so all players practice free-throws extensively. A team with a good *free-throw percentage* has a big advantage, not only because so many free-throw opportunities present themselves during a game but because intentional fouls in the final minutes of close games put players in foul-shooting situations.

When a player scores a 2-point field goal and is fouled in the process, he goes to the line for a single free-throw to try to complete a *3-point play*. (Be sure not to confuse this with the 3-point shot mentioned above.) The 3-point play generally gets the fans very excited. Even more exciting, but rarer, is the *4-point play* where a player is fouled as he is

Fig. 6: Standard free-throw set-up.

shooting a successful 3-point shot, and then makes the free-throw for a total of 4 points.

During the free-throw, players from both teams stand along either side of the *foul lane* to *rebound* any final free-throw that is missed, making sure not to step into the lane until the shooter *releases* the ball. (See **Fig. 6**) Players from both teams (6 in college, only 5 in the NBA), line up in alternating order, starting with the non-shooting team closest to the basket. Those players not lining up along the lane must stand 6 feet behind the free-throw line and 3 feet from the *foul circle*. A player who distracts the shooter commits a *free-throw lane violation*.

For a *technical* free-throw, only the shooter goes to the line. All the other players are required to stand behind him to limit potential distraction.

Basketball is a game of streaks with teams gaining momentum and often scoring several times in a row. When such a *run* occurs an announcer will point it out by saying, for example, "The Bulls are on a 10-2 run." This means that the Bulls scored 10 points while their opponents scored only 2 in the same period of time. For the Bulls to have scored 8 more points, their opponents must have missed several shots or committed *turnovers*.

Now let us see **HOW THE GAME IS PLAYED**.

HOW THE GAME IS PLAYED

The version of basketball played by professionals, colleges and high schools pits 5 players on each of 2 teams against each other. Yet the game can be played by just 2 players in what is called a game of *one-on-one*, while many informal and tournament matches are set up for *3-on-3*. Many of the sport's greatest players even practice daily for hours by themselves, sharpening their offensive skills against a lone *backboard*. Here we will explore the basics of basketball.

LENGTH OF GAME

A *regulation* game in professional basketball is divided into 4 *quarters* (or *periods*) of 12 minutes in length (college games consist of two 20-minute *halves*). A 15-minute *halftime* separates the first half from the second half. A brief 130-second break separates the 1st and 2nd, and the 3rd and 4th quarters. The *public address operator* will announce when there are only 2 minutes left in the game or any *overtime* period.

OVERTIME

When the score is tied at the end of a regulation game, additional 5-minute overtime (*OT*) periods are played until one team emerges victorious. A 1-minute separates the end of a regulation college game from its overtime, 100 seconds in the *NBA* (and between all subsequent OT periods). A *jump ball* is used to start each OT. As many OTs are played as are needed to break the tie. One college game between Bradley University and the University of Cincinnati in 1981 required 7 overtimes to decide the match in Cincinnati's favor. Teams do not switch sides for the overtime, but continue to play on the sides assigned in the second half.

CHOOSING SIDES

A team's *basket* is the one it scores into (the one in its *frontcourt*). The visiting team always gets to choose which basket it wants to shoot at for the first half. Teams then switch sides after the first half, and stay there even through any overtime periods.

OFFENSE VS. DEFENSE

During the game, one team or the other will have control or *possession* of the ball. The team that gains possession is on *offense* and has the opportunity to score *points*. The other team becomes the *defense* and tries to stop the offense from scoring. Their fans will start yelling "DE-FENSE" during a game to urge them to stop the offense. Both defensive and offensive players combine speed, grace, power and endurance to play the game. The specialized skills that must be developed to succeed in competitive basketball are discussed in greater detail in the chapter on **PLAYER SKILLS**.

During the action, when the ball is not controlled by either team it is called a *loose ball* and neither team is offense or defense. You can tell a ball is loose when you see many players scrambling to get a hold of the ball. As soon as one team controls the ball, it becomes the offense.

Offense

The offensive players move the ball toward their own basket by bouncing it (called *dribbling*) or *passing* it among themselves to get a good shot and score. The action is very rapid and may involve deceiving the defense to get by them. When a player with the ball moves very quickly toward the basket he is said to be *driving to the basket*.

Defense

The defense tries to prevent the offense from scoring by *guarding* it closely to force it to take difficult shots, by *blocking* these shots and by taking the ball away (called *steals*). When the offense loses possession through its own fault, it is called a *turnover* (although it is often a good defensive effort that throws the offense off-balance). Turnovers occur when the offense passes the ball *out of bounds* or commits a *floor violation*. A team that commits too many turnovers will often lose the game. It is easy to see how poorly a team is handling the ball when analysts list the number of turnovers each team has during the game.

THE JUMP BALL
Starting the Game
Two players, one from each team, start the game by jumping for a ball that an *official* tosses above them. For the initial jump ball (or the *tip-off*) each jumper must stand facing his basket with at least one foot inside the part of the *center circle* in his own *backcourt*. (See **Fig. 7**) The jumpers must also have both feet inside the *restraining circle* while their teammates must stand with both feet completely outside the restraining circle until one of the jumpers touches the ball.

The official then tosses the ball high above the heads of the jumpers and evenly between them. The jumpers cannot touch the ball until it has reached its highest point, so they actually tap it on its way down. One of the 2 jumpers must touch it before it reaches the floor or the official provides a new toss. Neither jumper can tap the ball more than twice or catch the ball himself. Also they must both stay completely inside the restraining circle until the ball has been tapped at least once.

Each jumper's goal is to tap the ball to one of his 4 teammates who try to gain possession of the ball, become the offense and try to score points. The players whose basket is nearest have first choice of position, although teammates cannot stand next to each other if an opponent wants to stand between them. In the NBA, if Team A wins the initial jump ball, Team B gets the ball to start the 2nd and 3rd quarters, while Team A starts the 4th. In college, the team that lost the tip-off gets the ball to start the second half.

Other Jump Ball Situations
In the NBA, jump balls are also used in certain situations other than for starting a period. The most common of these is when 2 opponents hold the ball simultaneously so

Fig. 7: Initial jump ball at center circle.

Fig. 8: A held ball.

that both have possession. This is called a *held ball* (See **Fig. 8**), and "tying up the ball" is frequently done on purpose when both teams are competing for a loose ball. To restart the action an official makes the 2 players that held the ball jump. If a shorter player must jump against a taller player (a *mismatch*) he will be at a disadvantage. However, just stopping the action and flow of the game can provide important strategic benefits to a team.

Other jump ball situations include when:
- a ball that went *out of bounds* was last touched by both teams simultaneously
- officials are unsure/disagree over which of 2 opposing players last touched a ball before it went out of bounds
- simultaneous *personal fouls* are committed by 2 opponents during a loose ball
- simultaneous *technical fouls* are committed by 2 opponents
- *double fouls* result from disagreement among officials
- a ball becomes *dead* during play through neither team's fault
- a ball becomes lodged between the basket and backboard
- starting any overtime period
- there is an inadvertent whistle by the officials

In all except the first 2 cases listed above, each team selects its best jumper (usually its tallest player on the floor) to take the jump at the center circle — just as they did for the tip-off. In the first two cases, the 2 players involved in the incident automatically become the designated jumpers — no matter what their size — at the circle closest to where the situation developed.

Possession Arrow
In college games, a *possession arrow* replaces the jump ball in the situations listed above to determine whose turn it is to throw the ball *inbounds*. The possession arrow is located near the *scorer's table*. After one team wins the tip-off, the arrow is set to give the other team possession after the next jump ball situation. The arrow changes on each subsequent jump ball situation, alternating which team gets possession for the *throw-in*. This is why it is also called the *alternating-possession rule*.

STOPPING PLAY

Play stops in basketball every time there is a *dead* ball.
Play is resumed by either a jump ball, a throw-in or a free-throw. The ball is considered dead in many situations,
such as:

- when a *floor violation*, personal foul or *fighting* foul is called
- after the first of multiple free-throws is taken
- after a successful field goal or final free-throw
- when time expires at the end of any period (a successful field goal counts if the ball leaves a shooter's hands before the buzzer sounds)
- when there is a held ball
- when the ball rests on the rim, gets lodged between basket and backboard, or goes over the top of backboard (See **Fig.** 9)
- after a technical free-throw is taken
- after any whistle by an official

RESTARTING PLAY

Live Ball

A ball is considered *live*
as soon as it is given to
the free-throw shooter,
the thrower on a throw-
in or when it is tossed up
by the official on a jump
ball. It becomes *alive*
only when it is released
by a shooter or thrower,
or legally tapped by a
jumper. The clock starts
only when the ball
becomes alive.

Fig. 9: A ball is dead if it goes behind the backboard.

Throw-in

After certain violations or fouls occur, the non-offending
team will restart the game by throwing in the ball from a
spot designated by an official. For the throw-in, one player
stands out-of-bounds at this spot and throws the ball to a
teammate standing in bounds. (See **Fig. 10**) The thrower
cannot hand the ball to the other player, throw it directly

into the basket or bounce it to a player, and he must get it to someone within 5 seconds or his team loses possession. The defense tries to prevent the thrower from getting the ball inbounds, especially toward the end of close games. A defender may not slap at the ball or knock it out of the thrower's hands, and he must allow the thrower room to maneuver in. If the offense is unable to complete the throw-in in time, it loses possession unless it uses a precious *timeout*.

Fig. 10: Throw-in.

THE CLOCKS

Time is very important in basketball. It affects almost everything players do — from how long players stand in one place, to how fast they try to get to a certain location, to the speed with which they must get a shot off.

Official Game Clock

The *official game clock* counts backwards to show how much time is left in each period (for example, if this clock says 5:31, that means 5 minutes and 31 seconds remain in the period). During the last minute of each period, the time is given with tenths-of-a-second intervals (e.g., 10.6 seconds remaining). This clock starts when a jump ball is legally tapped by one of the jumpers, the ball is legally touched by any inbounds player on a throw-in, a missed final free-throw attempt is touched by any player, or whenever an official signals to the *timer*.

The clock is stopped when an official blow his whistle because of:

- a personal foul, technical foul or floor violation
- a jump ball situation
- a *timeout* request
- an *official's timeout* for an emergency
- a need to confer with the other officials
- an unusual delay
- during the last minute of the 1st, 2nd and 3rd periods (both halves in college) following every successful field goal (no whistle)
- during the last 2 minutes of regulation or any OT periods following a successful field goal (no whistle)(NBA only)
- to signal an alternating-possession situation (college only)

Shot Clock (or 24-Second Clock)
There is also a *shot clock* to limit the length of time a team with the ball has to shoot it. In the NBA, this limit is 24 seconds so the shot clock is more commonly called the *24-second clock*. In college, a team now has 35 seconds (*35-second clock, 30-second clock* for women), although a *45-second clock* was used by men through the 1992-93 season. The shot clocks are usually located above each basket at the top of the backboard clearly visible to all players. In college arenas they are sometimes located in the corners of the floor instead.

Like the game clock, it counts down, showing how much time remains (e.g., 6 means the offensive team has 6 seconds left before the shot clock expires). If the clock reaches 0 before the offense takes a shot that either hits the rim or scores, the offense is penalized for a *24-second violation* (or *35-second violation*) and loses possession. As soon as the ball hits the rim or there is a change of possession, the clock is reset.

However, if the defense knocks the ball out of bounds and the offense retains possession, the offense takes the throw-in, but no time is added to the shot clock — it simply continues to play with just the unexpired time. Sometimes the defense will intentionally interfere with an offensive play to cause a throw-in situation that leaves the offense too little time to set up a good shot attempt. In college the offense gets either the unexpired time or a minimum of 5 seconds, so the officials may need to add a few seconds to the shot clock.

The 24-second clock was created to prohibit one team from keeping the ball for several minutes to prevent its opponent from scoring. This used to be a common tactic when one team was ahead near the end of the game, and it made the last few minutes boring for spectators, causing attendance to lag. In 1954, the NBA decided to limit the time a team could hold the ball, but it was unsure what amount of time was fair. Danny Biasone, owner of the Syracuse Nationals, suggested a logical way to determine this. By counting the average amount of time a basketball game took to play and dividing it by the average number of shots taken in a game, he concluded a basket was scored approximately every 18 seconds. A few seconds were added and the 24-second clock was born.

There are several other reasons to keep track of time in basketball. The officials count off 10 seconds in their heads for a player to get the ball from his backcourt across the *midcourt line* and 5 seconds for a throw-in. They also assure that no player spends more than 3 seconds in the key. These issues are discussed in the chapter on **VIOLATIONS AND FOULS.**

Restarting the Clocks
Whenever the game clock is stopped, so is the shot clock. The game clock starts again when the ball touches any player on the floor after a throw-in. After a free-throw, the game clock starts after the throw-in if the shot went in, or as soon as any player touches the ball after a final free-throw is missed. However, the shot clock only restarts when one team clearly gains possession of the ball. This is why there are times when the game clock is running and the shot clock has not yet been reset.

TIMEOUTS

Each team is given 7 opportunities, called full timeouts (each 100 seconds in length), in addition to one 20-second timeout for each half, to stop play. Teams use the time to rest and discuss strategy with their *coaches* and teammates by their bench. A team cannot use more than 4 full timeouts in the second half, and cannot *call* more than 3 in the last 2 minutes of regulation play. Leftover timeouts do not carry into overtime; instead 3 new full timeout opportunities are provided to each team for each overtime period with no restrictions as to when they can be called.

A team is *charged* (uses one up) with a timeout every time it requests one or whenever an official assigns it a *mandatory timeout*. There must be at least 2 timeouts called each period, so if neither team has taken one prior to 6:59 remaining in any quarter, the official *scorer* will charge the home team with a mandatory timeout at the first dead ball. If neither team calls a second timeout prior to 2:59 remaining in a quarter, the scorer again charges a mandatory timeout, this time to the visiting team.

After any timeout taken during the last 2 minutes of regulation or overtime, the offensive team has the option of taking its throw-in at midcourt instead of starting in the backcourt. This saves it the time and risk of bringing the ball the length of the court.

In men's college basketball there are usually 5 timeouts in a game (75 seconds each). During televised games, since 3 *commercial timeouts* are automatically provided (and not charged to any team), each team only gets to call 3 timeouts per game. In both televised and non-televised games, 1 additional timeout is given for each overtime period. Any timeouts not used in a period roll over into the next (including overtime). Starting in 1994-95, they will begin experimenting with one 20-second timeout per half, just like the NBA.

Timeouts can only be requested by a player on the floor when his team has possession of the ball, when the ball is dead, when an injured or disqualified player is being replaced, or when play has been stopped by the officials to correct a scoring error. The official must acknowledge the player's request to stop play. Coaches can signal to their players that they want them to call a timeout and come to the sidelines to talk things over, but they can not request the timeout themselves. Teams may also use a timeout to their advantage in certain key situations which are discussed in the chapter on **STRATEGY** (e.g., on a throw-in, to see how a team is set up, or to prevent a *5-second violation*).

In both college and pro games, if a player calls for a timeout when his team has none left, his team is assessed a technical foul. This can be a costly mistake for a player to make. During the Championship Game of the 1993 *NCAA Final Four*, *Chris Webber*, whose Michigan Wolverines were 2 points behind with 11 seconds left in the game, called for a timeout when his team had none left. A technical foul was called and the opponent, North Carolina, made both its foul shots and got the ball out of bounds, ultimately beating Michigan by a score of 77-71.

TIMEOUTS AND INJURIES
In the case of a serious *injury* or other emergency, college officials may use an *official timeout* to stop play and protect the player. In college, a timeout is not charged to the player's team if he is able to continue playing immediately, if he needs only to retrieve his glasses/contact lenses or if he is immediately *substituted* for. Officials will generally wait until the ball becomes dead or is in the control of the injured player's team before stopping play. This is to prevent a player from faking an injury to stop the opponent's momentum (e.g., *fast break* opportunity).

SUBSTITUTIONS

The first 5 players a team puts on the court is the *starting lineup*, usually consisting of its best players. Whenever a player needs to come out of the game, whether it is due to fatigue, injury, *foul trouble*, or the coach's desire to try a different approach, a substitute replaces him from the *bench*.

Any substitute must first report to the *scorer's table* to give his name and number, and that of the player he is replacing. He must then sit in the *substitution box* located in front of that table to wait for the next dead ball. He can only come onto the floor after the horn has blown and an official beckons him in. Substitutions can be made during timeouts and in between periods without waiting (except during the last 15 seconds of a college timeout). Free-throw shooters and jumpers involved in a jump ball cannot be substituted for unless they are injured. In such a case, the coach of the opposing team selects the replacement player.

A recent NBA rule passed in response to concerns about *infection control* requires the officials to remove any player who is bleeding, no matter how minor the cut or wound. As soon as the official can stop play, this player is removed and a substitute is sent in immediately. Before stopping play, officials will wait until a bleeding player has taken his free-throws or competed for a jump ball, and they will not interrupt a fast break opportunity. The player's team may choose to take a timeout instead of sending a substitute in, especially if the bleeding player can be attended to quickly. As soon as the player's wound is dressed to prevent the contamination of others, he may return to the game.

Now that you have an understanding of the procedures used in running an organized basketball game, let us learn about the **PLAYER SKILLS** needed in competitive basketball.

PLAYER SKILLS

Basketball players utilize the most basic athletic skills: running, jumping and handling a ball. These must be combined to develop *offensive* skills (*dribbling, shooting, pivoting, faking* and *passing*), *defensive* skills (*guarding, blocking* and *stealing*), and general skills (*rebounding* and *screening*). Each of these is discussed more fully below.

OFFENSIVE TEAM SKILLS
Passing
A pass is when one player throws the ball to a teammate. In general, the purpose of passing is to move the ball to get around *defenders* and score. Specifically, passing is used to:
- start a play
- move the ball down the court and closer to the basket
- get the ball to an *open* player (without defenders nearby) who is better skilled and/or in a better position to score
- avoid losing the ball (*turnover*) to a persistent defender

Any pass is successful if it gets to a teammate (the *receiver*) without being stolen by the opponent and improves the offense's position. The best passers have good *court vision*, meaning they are able to anticipate how plays will develop and determine where a receiver will become open. Since his teammates are in constant motion, a passer needs to throw the ball where he thinks a receiver is headed, called *leading* the receiver. Accuracy is critical because an imprecise pass is more easily stolen by an opponent. Good passes reach receivers at waist level or in their hands if they are ready to shoot. When a receiver makes a basket immediately after a pass, the passer is credited with an *assist*.

The area where a pass travels between the passer and the receiver is called the *passing lane*. An opposing player may *step into the passing lane* in an effort to *cut off a pass* and either deflect or *steal* the ball. To keep defenders off-balance, ball handlers use a variety of passes depending on the situation:

Chest Pass — this 2-handed pass is the most common and quickest, used when there is no obstacle between the passer and receiver (usually around the *perimeter*). The ball is held to the chest and released with a flick of the wrists towards the receiver's chest.

Bounce Pass — the ball is bounced about 2/3 of the way to the receiver. (See **Fig. 11**) Although it takes longer than a chest pass, it is more effective in a crowd of defenders. There are 2 versions — the 2-handed type is a chest pass with a bounce, while the 1-handed version is used to get around a defender by extending the arm to one side and releasing the ball with a flick of the wrist.

Baseball Pass (*Outlet* or *Full-Court Pass*) — named because its motion resembles that of a baseball player throwing, this 1-handed pass is used to traverse the length of the court, usually after a *defensive rebound*. The ball is thrown from above and behind the passer's shoulder to a receiver near the opposite basket. Though this pass is difficult to control and easy to intercept, it is the best for distance and is essential to starting the *fast break*.

Fig. 11: A bounce pass.

Overhead Pass — this 2-handed pass is similar to the chest pass except the ball is held over and slightly behind the passer's head, then quickly tossed over a defender's reach. (See **Fig. 12**). It is used by a player to get the ball over a defender closely guarding him, to reach a teammate under the basket or to initiate the fast break.

Fig. 12: An overhead pass.

Flick Pass (*Sidearm Pass*) — this rapid 1-handed pass from shoulder height often follows a fake. Its quick motion is designed to get the ball through an obstacle.

Thread-the-Needle Pass — a type of flick pass where the ball is squeezed through a narrow gap between 2 or more defenders to a receiver usually positioned under the basket, much as thread would go through the eye of a needle.

Behind the Back Pass — though rarely used because it is risky, this 1-handed waist-level pass behind the passer's back to a nearby receiver often catches defenders by surprise.

Lob Pass — this high-arcing 2-handed pass is aimed over the head of a receiver in mid-stride so he does not have to stop on his way to the basket. Also used to reach a tall teammate under the basket.

Touch Pass (*Tap* or *Bat Pass*) — this difficult maneuver requiring good court vision occurs when a receiver, instead of catching a pass, merely deflects it with his fingertips to a more open teammate

While passing is an extremely important skill, it is not the only way a team can move the ball or get by a defender. Another method is by dribbling.

OFFENSIVE INDIVIDUAL SKILLS
Dribbling
Dribbling is used to move a ball down the court, evade a defender, *drive* to the basket or set up a play. A player with the ball <u>cannot</u> run or walk without dribbling it. Dribbling is simply when a player continuously bounces the ball on the floor using his fingers and fingertips. He can be running, walking or even standing still as he dribbles. A *dribble series* ends when the ball handler allows the ball to rest in both his hands, shoots, passes, loses the ball or stops bouncing it. When dribbling, players always look ahead to survey the floor, never down at the ball.

The ball handler needs to follow certain rules while dribbling. He must:
- use only 1 hand at a time (but he can alternate hands)
- dribble only 1 series at a time — he cannot start, stop and start (or it is called a *double dribble*)
- take only 1 step for each bounce of the ball, unless he is shooting a *layup* (though this is rarely enforced)
- not use his palm to slap or carry the ball

The ball handler must be careful to maintain control of the ball between bounces since defenders will be trying to steal the ball away. Fast dribbles close to the floor allow for greater ball control. High, slow dribbles are used to travel long distances down the court. A good dribbler is able to change the pace of his dribble to be less predictable and change hands (e.g., *crossover dribble*) or directions quickly. He can move the ball straight ahead, backwards, left, right, behind his back or between his legs.

Faking

Throughout a game, players are always trying to deceive their opponents into thinking they are going to do one thing when they actually do another. These are called *fakes* or *feints*. Any part of the body can be used, including the eyes, to confuse a defender. For example, a player can pretend to shoot but dribble by his opponent, pretend to pass in one direction then pass in another, take a step right and dribble left, and so on. A *head fake* is one of the most effective, where a player moves his head as if he is going to shoot the ball but does not shoot, causing a defender to jump too early. It is a constant challenge for opponents to keep up.

Shooting

Shooting is how teams score points and win games. Shooters need good hand-eye coordination to place the ball in the basket. However, *shot selection* is just as crucial. Players should only *release* their shot when they are in good shooting position (facing the basket or *squaring up*) and within their own personal *shooting range*. A shooter's job is made more difficult because defenders try to prevent him from doing this by trying to *block* his shot (interfering with it by touching or *getting a piece of the ball* on its way to the basket). The best shooters are adept at faking, using their eyes, head and entire body to get clear of defenders. Shots that look erratic are often desperate last-second attempts before the *shot clock* runs out.

Good shooters propel the ball with the fingertips of one hand only, imparting a slight backspin to the ball. Most also shoot the ball high into the air with an arc, so it will go over the *rim* more easily. Players who are able to provide the right combination of spin and arc are said to have a "soft touch". Even inaccurate shots thrown with a soft touch may score if they bounce lightly off the rim and into the basket, called a *shooter's roll*.

While players can be as creative as they like in shooting, some of the most common shots taken are:

Jump Shot — a player jumps up and shoots the ball while in mid-air. (See **Fig. 13**) Before his shot, the ball rests in the palms and fingers of his shooting hand and is supported by the other hand. It is then propelled by the fingertips in an arc toward the basket. He must release the ball before he lands or he is called for *traveling*. It is the most widely used shot, popular because it allows a player to shoot over taller defenders, or to change his mind at the last minute and pass to a more open teammate (called a *jump pass*). The jump shot is especially effective when combined with a head fake, since a slight deceptive delay before jumping may cause a defender to jump too early. There are also turn-around jumpers which surprise the opposition. Today, players have increased the range of this shot up to 30 feet from the basket, making it an even more dangerous weapon.

Set Shot — same as the jump shot except it is taken from a standing position, with both feet firmly planted on the floor during the release, usually 20 feet or more from the basket. Today it is used less often, but is still important since most *free-throws* are set shots.

Free-throw or *foul shot* — a set shot taken from the *foul line* with no one guarding the shooter. Players make a higher percentage of these than regular set shots because there are no defenders to distract them. The shooter can take up to 10 seconds to release the ball; often he bounces the ball several times, choosing where to place his hands before shooting. *Rick Barry*, the best free-throw shooter of all-time, used a 2-handed underhanded foul shot which is rarely used today. A team's free-throw shooting can greatly affect the outcome of the game (See the chapters on **SCORING** and **STRATEGY** for more information.)

Layup (*Layin*) — the shot with the greatest chance for success (the highest percentage shot). It is taken from very close range and banked off the *backboard* so it drops into the basket for a layup (or sometimes the ball is just dropped into the basket for a layin — though these terms are used interchangeably today). (See **Fig. 14**) Players usually take layups on the run (off the dribble), jumping off one foot to get the ball as close to the basket as possible. This shot is used whenever the shooter has a clear path to the basket and is commonly used to finish a *fast break*.

Reverse layup — one of several creative variations of the layup where a player drives toward the basket, passes under it and shoots the ball from the other side of the rim using either hand.

Hook Shot — one of the most difficult shots to make and to defend against, this is a favorite of players in the *low post* position. Both the basket and the defender are behind the shooter when he releases the ball. The ball is held chest high

| Fig. 13: A jump shot. | Fig. 14: A layup. |

with both hands as the player pivots and extends one arm up in a sweeping motion toward the basket before releasing the ball. *Kareem Abdul-Jabbar* made famous a version of this dubbed the *skyhook*, a shot that was impossible to block since he was 7'2" tall.

Dunk (*Slam dunk*, Jam or Stuff) — when a player in close proximity to the basket jumps and strongly throws the ball down into it (See **Fig. 15**). A player is only permitted to hang on the rim after dunking to prevent injury to himself or others. Dunks are often the most athletic and creative of shots (sometimes thrown backwards and over the head) and are a favorite of tall, physical players. The dunk is often used to intimidate opponents, or to "fire up" (instill excitement among) spectators and teammates experiencing a temporary slump. It is during this shot that a backboard may shatter. Banned in the college game from 1968-1976, the dunk's critics point to missed scoring opportunities when a *hotdogging* (showoff) player forgoes an easy layup for a dunk and then misses it.

Fig. 15: A slam dunk.

Tip in — a one-handed deflection used mostly by tall players to redirect an off-target shot by a teammate into the basket.

Alley-oop — an acrobatic play where a passer lobs the ball to a teammate who snags it in mid-air and dunks it in one motion. It requires an accurate pass and perfect timing.

Pivoting

A player holding the ball (either because he has just received a pass or has stopped dribbling,) is permitted to rotate in any direction with one stepping foot, as long any part of his other foot (called his *pivot* foot) remains touching the floor. This ability of a player to turn quickly on one foot is important in passing and shooting, and to prevent *traveling* violations. The pivot foot is always the first foot a player lands on while catching the ball, but if he lands on both feet simultaneously, he can choose which foot to swivel on.

Screening

A *screen* is set when an offensive player uses his body to create an obstacle for the defense while allowing a teammate to get open or closer to the basket. A player setting a screen (or setting a *pick*) must be stationary or a *blocking foul* is called against him. A defensive player needs to beware of the opposing team's screen because if he runs into it he may lose the player he was guarding or be called for *charging*. This offensive player would then be free to receive a pass or drive to the basket.

CROSSOVER SKILLS: OFFENSIVE AND DEFENSIVE

Rebounding

Rebounding is the one skill that is used both on offense and on defense. A *rebound* is when a player recovers a missed shot at the basket. When a player rebounds a shot missed by a teammate, it is called an *offensive rebound*. If the same player who took the shot gets the rebound it is said that "he got his own rebound." When the shot was missed by a member of the opposing team, it is called a *defensive rebound*. It is easier to get defensive rebounds than offensive rebounds. The team that controls the rebounding very often wins the game. Players try to position their bodies between their opponents and the basket, called *boxing out*. The best rebounders are strong, tall and have good jumping ability, although any players who know how to box out well can get rebounds. Just as important as these physical attributes are good timing and the ability to anticipate where the ball will go after it hits the backboard or rim.

DEFENSIVE INDIVIDUAL SKILLS

The goal of defenders is to prevent the offense from scoring
and to create turnovers (See **HOW THE GAME IS PLAYED**).

<u>Guarding</u>

Defensive players *guard* opponents by following them
around the court to prevent them from driving towards the
basket, taking open shots or making easy passes to
teammates. A defensive player uses quick footwork to keep
his body between his opponent and the basket, and usually
holds his hands up in the air to interfere with passes and
shots. However, the defender may not use physical contact to
impede the movement of an opponent unless he has already
established his position (see *blocking* in **VIOLATIONS & FOULS**
chapter). Although it is illegal, officials usually allow a slight
amount of hand-to-body contact, called *handchecking*. (See
Fig. 16)

Fig. 16: Handchecking a player.

Shot Blocking

Shot blocking is an attempt by a defensive player to stop an offensive player's shot attempt with his hand. (See **Fig. 17**) Any deflection of a shot, no matter how slight, usually sends it off its intended course, preventing a basket. However, if a defender swipes at the ball but instead hits his opponent's arm or otherwise touches his body, the defender could be called for a foul. The one exception to this is that a defender can legally touch a shooter's hand while it is on the ball because the hand is considered part of the ball. Good shot blockers have long arms, strong jumping ability and good timing to meet a shooter in mid-air.

Fig. 17: Shot block attempt.

Steals

Whenever a defender gets the ball by intercepting a pass or dislodging a dribbled ball, it is called a steal. The best players at stealing anticipate the next offensive action and move rapidly to recover the ball. Since a steal happens so quickly, it often allows the player who has stolen the ball to get a head-start toward his own basket where he can likely score unopposed. In such a case, not only did the steal prevent the offense from scoring 2 points, but it resulted in 2 points for the team that was on defense. This is called a *4-point turnaround* (2+2=4).

We are now ready to examine some of the **PLAYER POSITIONS** that use these skills.

PLAYER POSITIONS

In organized basketball there are always 5 players on the court per team — generally 2 *forwards*, a *center* and 2 *guards*. *Pick-up* games can be played with less than 5 players to a side. The best basketball players today are well-versed in all the skills we just reviewed in the chapter on **PLAYER SKILLS**, yet each of the 5 main player positions require a different mix of these as well as distinct physical attributes. Each player generally guards an opponent that plays the same position. Since possession can change at any moment, all the players must be prepared to switch from offense to defense and back.

In addition to the *starting lineup* (the 5 *starters* who are generally also the team's best players) a team's *bench* (all its other players) is also important to its overall success. In the *NBA*, each team is allowed to have a maximum of 12 active players on its *roster*. Since injuries are common, a team may have less than 12 players to rotate in, so it is best served by having several strong *substitutes* for all positions. (Although college teams are not limited in size, only 13 scholarships are available for men's teams, 15 for women.)

Each NBA team is permitted to have one player *captain* and up to 2 co-captains. The captain is the only player who can talk to an *official* during a *timeout*, and then only to discuss a rule interpretation. No player may ever question an official's judgment. The captain acts on behalf of the coach who cannot be on the court. Today, coaches constantly talk to their players on the court, but at one time this was not permitted. Nat Holman, a coach at City College of N.Y. (*CCNY*) in the 1950s, actually learned to be a ventriloquist so when he threw his voice it seemed his players were getting suggestions from fans in the stands!

GUARDS
The guards (*ball handlers*) tend to be the smallest and fastest members of the team, and they lead the offense by

handling the ball and calling the plays. They need to be excellent *dribblers* because they start almost every play in the *backcourt* and must successfully move the ball into the *frontcourt*. Since they play the furthest away from the basket (covering the middle and backcourt) they must also be great *passers* to get the ball to teammates who are closer, or they must develop good outside *shooting* skills. Most of the best *3-point shooters* are guards. Guards sometimes rebound, but not as often as forwards or centers.

There are 2 types of guards with different functions; both types are represented on the floor at a time:

Point Guard (Lead guard, Number 1 guard, *Playmaker*) — the best ball handler on the team, he controls the ball more than any of his teammates. As the extension of the team's coach, he makes decisions on the floor which generate the team's offense, taking advantage of his teammates' strengths to create *scoring opportunities*. To make these decisions, it is important for him to have good *court vision* (the ability to see the entire floor to determine the position of teammates and defenders) as he dribbles the ball down the court. He uses hand signals to communicate the chosen plays to his teammates. Teammates usually try to get the ball back to the point guard whenever the defense breaks up one of their offensive attempts so that he can set them up again.

Shooting Guard (Second Guard, Off Guard, Number 2 Guard) — he is usually a reliable outside (*perimeter*) shooter quick at penetrating the defense and *driving to the basket* to score. Generally the shooting guard is also a talented dribbler and ball handler, though not as gifted as the point guard. On some teams his position can also be played by a small forward (or *swing man*).

FORWARDS
The forwards are bigger than the guards but smaller than the center, and they are commonly the team's highest scorers. On both offense and defense, they play near the

corners of the court on either side of the basket, taking jump shots, driving to the basket and rebounding. A team's 2 forwards serve different functions — one is more of a roaming shooter and the other is more of a rebounder:

Small Forward (Quick Forward) — he is often the most versatile player on a team, combining the quickness, agility and ball-handling skills of a guard with the physical strength to jostle under the basket and score amid large defenders. His skills include solid shooting from both the perimeter and close range, the ability to drive to the basket, and rebounding on both ends of the court. He is also the third player to join the guards on a *fast break*, so he is pivotal in the transition game.

Power Forward (Big Forward, Strong Forward) — the less agile and swift of the forwards, he is often interchangeable with the center. This player uses his height and strength primarily for defense and rebounding at both ends of the court. Offensively, he scores by making shots from close to the basket, and he also sets *screens* to free up his teammates for shots. The best power forwards are effective in both the *low post* and *high post* (**Fig. 18**), able to shoot while facing the basket or with their backs to it (called *posting up*).

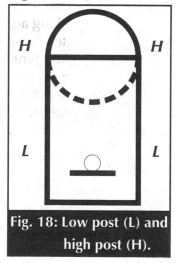

Fig. 18: Low post (L) and high post (H).

CENTER

The center (also called the *pivot* because many plays are created around him) is usually the tallest, biggest and strongest player on a team. Most professional centers are 7' or taller, making them intimidating forces. Among his tasks, the traditional center lists rebounding, blocking shots and screening. Most centers are also adept at shooting close to the basket or with their backs to it, and may develop a hook shot from as far as 15' away which is very difficult to defend. Today's centers (especially some European players) have far greater skills than their counterparts did 10 years ago — they can run, dribble and even shoot from the outside.

Despite this increased versatility in modern day players, a center's primary position on the court is still closest to the basket, where he is able to *tip in* missed shots, receive passes from other teammates for easier shots to the basket, and rebound. It is important for him to have "good hands" (strong and reliable) to handle rebounds and passes. On occasion, a team will choose to replace the center, playing with 3 forwards/2 guards or 3 guards/2 forwards instead.

THE BENCH

The bench is a team's reserve, used by the coach to relieve his starters when they are tired or in *foul trouble*, or to change an offensive or defensive style of play. Since coaches put on the floor combinations of players who work well together, more than one substitution is often made at a time or in quick succession. The more talented substitute players a team has, the deeper is its bench. Yet it is difficult to find players who are consistent coming off the bench because they enter the game cold. A good substitute, however, must be able to get in the game and have an immediate impact, often for just a short period of time.

The best substitute on a team is called the *sixth man*. He is likely to be the first substitute brought into a game when the team needs a fresh player to do one or more of the following:
- change the pace of the game
- provide some offensive points
- throw off the opposition's offense off with some overpowering defensive skills
- take control of the ball with strong rebounding

The behavior of all players is controlled by **THE OFFICIALS**.

THE OFFICIALS

Three *officials* control the conduct of a basketball game: a *crew chief*, *referee* and *umpire*. College games use either 2 or 3: the referee and 1 or 2 umpires. They are all responsible for calling *fouls* and *violations*, indicating successful *field goals*, pointing to the location for *throw-ins* and inspecting all the equipment. Official *scorers* and *timers* assist them. All the officials have *elastic power* which is the authority to make immediate decisions on anything not specifically covered in the rules. Whenever officials are unsure about a decision, they confer with each other.

When a foul or violation occurs, the official who sees it blows his whistle to stop play and signals the timekeeper to stop the *official game clock*. For *personal fouls*, the official also tells the scorer the offending player's *uniform* number, and then puts up his fingers to show the number of *free-throws* to be taken. More of the signals officials use to communicate with each other and the players are illustrated in **OFFICIALS' HAND SIGNALS** at the end of the book.

CREW CHIEF
The head official in charge of a game is the crew chief, selected because he is the best and usually the most experienced official on the floor. Although the nearest official signals when a field goal is scored, it is the crew chief who makes the ultimate decision on whether or not a basket will count. He also decides all matters on which the other officials, scorers or timers disagree. In college games, the head official is the referee and he has similar duties to the crew chief, except he may not set aside or question another official's decision.

REFEREES AND UMPIRES
The next best official in a game is the referee while the umpire is generally the official with the least experience.

SCOREKEEPERS

The scorer and his assistants sit at the *scorers' table*, located behind one of the sidelines, to keep the game's official scorebook. In this book, they record all *timeouts*, field goals made and missed, free-throws made and missed, and keep a summary of points scored. In addition to keeping count of all *team fouls*, they also record all personal and *technical fouls* called against each player and notify the officials when a player has 6 (5 in college) and needs to be removed from the game. To do their job, they keep track of the names, uniform numbers and positions of all the players in the game, and must be notified of the starting lineup and any *substitutions* made throughout the game. Every player that enters the game must first report to the scorers' table. The scorers provide summary score sheets to the media during the game and send a final game report to the *NBA*.

TIMERS

Two timers also sit at the scorers' table and record all playing time and stoppages in the game. One operates the official game clock, stopping it every time an official blows the whistle and restarting it when the official signals him to do so. The second timer operates the *shot clock*. A separate stopwatch is used during timeouts, called the *timeout watch*.

TELEVISION REPLAYS

College officials may use replay equipment or television monitors only to determine which individuals participated in a fight, to rectify a timer's or scorer's error, or to fix any problem relating to a malfunctioning of the clocks. They cannot, however, rely on such outside sources for assistance in determining *goaltending*, *basket interference*, field goals, fouls or anything else.

The next chapter discusses the **VIOLATIONS & FOULS** these officials look for.

VIOLATIONS & FOULS

Basketball games are played in a relatively small area, especially when you consider the height and weight of the players involved. Each shot attempt concentrates most of these players into an even smaller space beneath the basket. As they battle for control of the ball, contact between them is frequent and often against the rules, so *officials* call only the most severe fouls. It is impossible for the officials to catch every violation, some infractions are difficult for them to detect (e.g., *palming*), and sometimes they even ignore incidental minor contact so the flow of the game is not disrupted.

There are 3 categories of violations or fouls: *floor violations*, *personal fouls* and *technical fouls*. When a player commits an infraction in handling the ball or by his position on the court, it is called a floor violation. Violations do not cause harm to any opponent nor do they prevent an opposing player's movement on the court. Personal fouls, on the other hand, are called for contact between players that may result in injury or which provide one team with an unfair advantage. All the personal fouls committed by members of a team are also counted collectively as *team fouls*. Technical fouls are called for some procedural violations and misconduct that officials believe are detrimental to the game.

When an official sees a foul or rule violation committed, he will blow his whistle to stop play and the game clock is stopped. He then identifies the foul or violation with a hand signal (See **OFFICIALS' HAND SIGNALS**) and enforces the penalty. The penalty for committing a foul or violation is to award the wronged team *free-throws* and/or the opportunity to throw the ball back *inbounds*. When a violation is committed by the offense, there is a change of possession as the defense inbounds the ball by a *throw-in*. If the violation was committed by the defense, the offense is either awarded free-throws or retains possession for the throw-in.

TABLE 1: SUMMARY OF PENALTIES

KEY: FT = Free-Throw; * = if the last FT is successful the opponent will throw in the ball

EVENT	NBA		College	
	Offensive	Defensive	Offensive	Defensive
Floor Violation	Throw-in by defense	Throw-in by offense	Throw-in by defense	Throw-in by offense
Shooting Foul	Not applicable	1 FT by offense if shot was successful* OR 2 FTs by offense if shot was unsuccessful* OR 3 FTs by offense if 3-point shot was unsuccessful* (proposed)	Not applicable	1 FT by offense if shot was successful* OR 2 FTs by offense if shot was unsuccessful* OR 3 FTs by offense if 3-point shot was unsuccessful*
Non-Shooting Foul	Throw-in by defense	If 4 or less team fouls: throw-in by offense / If over the limit (5 or more team fouls): 2 FTs by offense*	Throw-in by defense	If 6 or less team fouls: throw-in by offense / If over the limit (7 to 9 team fouls): 1-and-1 by offense* OR If over the limit (10 or more team fouls): 2 FTs by offense*
Flagrant Foul	2 FTs and throw-in by defense	1 FT and throw-in by offense on a shooting foul where offense's shot was successful / 2 FTs and throw-in by offense if shot was unsuccessful or for any other foul	2 FTs and throw-in by defense	2 FTs and throw-in by offense
Technical Foul	1 FT and throw-in by the team that had possession at time the technical was committed	1 FT and throw-in by the team that had possession at time the technical was committed	2 FTs and throw-in by defense	2 FTs and throw-in by offense
Away-From-the-Play Foul	1 FT and throw-in by defense	1 FT and throw-in by offense	Not applicable	Not applicable

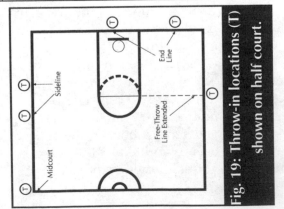

Labels: Midcourt, Sideline, End Line, Free-Throw Line Extended

Fig. 19: Throw-in locations (T) shown on half court.

PENALTIES

The penalty for each violation or foul is summarized in **Table 1.**

Throw-In

When an official determines that a violation or non-shooting foul occurred, the ball is considered *dead* and the wronged team restarts the game by throwing in the ball from the spot he designates. (See chapter on **HOW THE GAME IS PLAYED**). **Fig. 19** shows the various inbounding locations from which a throw-in can be taken.

Shooting Free-Throws

In certain instances, the commission of a foul by a team allows a player from the opposing team to go to the free-throw line. The number of free-throw opportunities awarded depends on the type of foul that was committed. When a player *in the act of shooting* is fouled, it is called a *shooting foul*. It does not matter if the shot had no chance of going into the basket or if the official blew his whistle before the ball left a shooter's hands. Since officials subjectively determine whether or not a player was in the act of shooting, ball handlers who see that they are about to be fouled often make a last second attempt to shoot just to get to the line.

The following scenarios (summarized in **Table 1**) are possible:
- 1 Free-throw: awarded when a shooting foul is committed on a player whose shot was successful. This sets up a potential *3-point play* (or the very rare *4-point play* if the successful basket was a *3-point shot*).
- 2 Free-throws: awarded when a player is fouled while shooting and misses the shot. Awarded for *non-shooting fouls* when the fouling team is *over the limit* in team fouls (discussed below).
- *1-and-1*: in college only, where the second free-throw is only taken if the first attempt was successful. Awarded for non-shooting fouls when the fouling team is over the limit in team fouls.

- 1 or 2 Free-throws <u>and</u> the ball out of bounds: awarded for a *flagrant foul* on any player (with or without the ball); the fouled team keeps possession of the ball after shooting the free-throw(s).
- 3 Free-throws: awarded only in college games, if a player is fouled in the act of shooting from behind the *3-point line*
- 1 Technical Free-throw: awarded to a team for any technical foul committed by its opponents, it is taken by the team's best free-throw shooter. In college, 2 technical free-throws are taken and the fouled team then gets possession.

VIOLATIONS

Through the 1950s, basketball games suffered from low scores because there were no rules to prevent one player from controlling the ball for long periods of time. Since fans quickly became bored with these tactics, rules were created to increase the pace of the game. The most common violations are discussed below in alphabetical order:

- *Backcourt Violation* — once the offense brings the ball into its *frontcourt*, it cannot go into the backcourt with it unless an opponent causes it to go there through a deflection or other interference. Sometimes a player gives up pursuing a *loose ball* that is rolling towards his backcourt because he knows even if he catches up to it, his team will lose possession of the ball for this violation. A throw-in from the *midcourt line* into the backcourt is permitted.

- *Double Dribble* — is called when a dribbling player picks up the ball with one or both hands and then commences dribbling again. A player may dribble for a second time if a *field goal* attempt first touches the *rim* or *backboard*, or if his first dribble ended involuntarily (such as if a pass or fumble is touched by another player, or when an opponent causes the ball handler to lose control of the ball).

- *Five Seconds* (college only) — occurs when a ball handler holds the ball for 5 seconds while an opponent is within 6 feet of him.

- *Free-Throw Lane Violation* — players lined up along the *foul lane* during a free-throw attempt may not step into the lane until the shooter has released the ball. If an offensive player steps in, the free-throw is forfeited and the defense gets the ball out of bounds; if a defensive player steps in, the free-throw counts if it was good or is rethrown.

- *Illegal Assist in Scoring* — a player cannot use the rim or the backboard to lift himself up and score. Similarly, a player cannot assist another player in scoring by giving him extra height.

- *Isolation* — the offense cannot position 3 or more players above the tip of the free-throw circle on the *weakside* (the side away from the ball) (*NBA* only)

- *Kicked* or *Punched Ball* — a defensive player cannot intentionally kick, knee or punch a ball.

- Palming — a ball handler cannot dribble the ball using his palm or carry it in his palm. Though often done by players, palming is difficult to detect so officials rarely enforce it.

- *Swinging Elbows* — excessive or vigorous swinging of the elbows by a ball handler holding the ball near a defensive player, even if there is no contact.

- *Ten-Second Violation* — from the moment the ball is touched by an inbounds player on the throw-in in the backcourt, the offensive team has only 10 seconds to cross the midcourt line into the frontcourt. This rule was added in 1932 to increase the game's tempo, prevent stalling, decrease keepaway games and encourage full-court defense. The only exceptions to this rule are in the event of:

- a kicked or punched ball
- a technical foul or *delay of game* warning against the defense
- suspension of play by an official for *infection control* (e.g., if a player is bleeding)

- *Three-Second Violation* — No offensive player can stand in the *foul lane* (or the imaginary 4' area extending out of bounds from it behind the basket) for more than 3 seconds. A player in the act of shooting can, however, finish his shot even if the 3 seconds expires. The count starts only when the ball is in the offense's frontcourt. A player can step out of the key and back in to give himself a new 3-second count. This rule prevents offensive players from stationing themselves below the basket waiting for a pass and an easy scoring opportunity, and forces players to stay in constant motion, creating more excitement.

- *Throw-In Violation* — a player must release the ball within 5 seconds of when an official gives it to him to start a throw-in. He also may not step on any part of a boundary line before he releases the ball.

- *Traveling* (*Walking* or Too Many Steps) — Traveling occurs when the ball handler takes more than one step without dribbling or releasing the basketball for a pass or shot. A player who is standing still when he receives a pass must keep his *pivot foot* on the floor until he is ready to dribble, shoot or pass the ball, whereas, a player who is moving when the ball comes to him can take a maximum of 2 steps in coming to a stop, passing or shooting. If a player falls with the ball he cannot slide. Also, a player may not catch his own missed shot before it touches the backboard, rim or another player. Traveling is one of the most overlooked violations in the *NBA*.

- *Twenty-Four Second Violation* — the offense must attempt a field goal within 24 seconds of gaining possession of the ball (35 seconds for college). If the ball has left a shooter's hands when the shot clock expires and it touches the rim of the basket, there is no violation and play can continue without a throw-in; if the ball goes into the basket, the field goal counts.

- *Other violations*
  - The ball cannot enter the basket from below or it will go to the opponents.
  - A player cannot step out of bounds on his way to setting up a *screen*.

One type of violation is unique in that points are scored without the ball even going through the basket:

- *Goaltending* — if a defensive player touches a ball that is in the basket, partially in the area above the basket (the *cylinder*), or on its way down in its trajectory toward the basket (See **Fig. 20**) a 2-point field goal is automatically awarded to the offense. Touching the ball by putting a hand up through the basket ring or trapping the ball against the backboard are also goaltending. Generally, officials only call this if there was a chance for the

CYLINDER

Fig. 20: Goaltending or basket interference.

ball to go into the basket without the interference. Only one point is awarded if the interference occurs during a free-throw attempt; 3 points if it occurs during a 3-point try.

- *Basket Interference* — similar to goaltending except it is committed by an offensive player at his own basket and points are not automatically awarded. Instead, any basket scored is <u>not</u> counted and the opponents take possession for a throw-in. An offensive player is not called for interference for touching the ball in the cylinder if he is holding on to it for a shot, such as a *dunk*.

PERSONAL AND TEAM FOULS

Personal fouls can be called against an offensive or defensive player at any time during the game, including when the ball is dead. These fouls impose penalties for breaking the rules during the game. The NBA or *NCAA* may also impose additional fines or suspensions after a game. In general, a player on the court cannot push, hold, trip, elbow, restrain, hack or charge into his opponents. One important exception is that contact with the hand of an offensive player while it is touching the ball is not illegal because his hand is considered part of the ball. Most officials also overlook *incidental contact* and allow a minimal amount of hand-to-body contact by the defender.

<u>Keeping Track of Personal and Team Fouls</u>
Each personal foul committed by a player is counted toward that player's total foul tally and his team's total foul tally. For example, the announcer will say *"Patrick Ewing* has just committed his 3rd personal foul. It is the Knicks' 6th team foul."

Since it is inevitable that contact will occur between players in the heat of battle and since players also commit fouls for strategic reasons (such as to prevent opponents from *freezing* the ball near the end of the game), a player is not disqualified from continuing to play in a game until he has committed 6 personal fouls (5 in college). It is common for a coach to insert a temporary substitute for a key player in *foul trouble* (usually one who has 4 or more fouls, or who has picked up 2 or 3 fouls early in the game).

Once a player *fouls out*, a substitute must take his place for the rest of the game.

Over the Limit in Team Fouls

When a team commits 5 or more team fouls per *period* (4 or more fouls in each *overtime*) that team is *over the limit*. Any additional non-shooting foul committed by that team will send the opponents to the free-throw line for 2 attempts instead of just awarding it with a throw-in. If a team is able to complete the first 10 minutes of a period (or 3 minutes of overtime) without going over the limit, it is allowed to incur 1 team foul in the last 2 minutes of the period without penalty (see *Away-From-The-Play Foul* below). In college, when a team has committed 7 or more fouls in any half, the opposing team goes to the line for a 1-plus-1 opportunity (if the first free-throw is missed, there is no second throw). After a team commits 10 fouls in a half, the opponents get to shoot 2 free throws regardless of whether they make the first one or not.

Fig. 21: Charging or blocking foul.

Types of Personal Fouls

A player cannot be guilty of a personal foul if he maintains his verticality. This means that he "owns" the space directly above him but he cannot lean into or reach over an opponent. There are several categories of behavior players cannot engage in, the most common of which are described here in alphabetical order:

- *Blocking, Illegal* — when a defensive player has <u>not</u> *established his position* (does not have his feet firmly planted on the floor before the offensive player's head and shoulder get past him) and interferes with a ball handler's straight line movement. Defenders may also not use a hip movement that delays or prevents an opponent from moving. Blocking is the reverse of *charging*. (See **Fig. 21**)

- Charging — this is an offensive foul where a ball handler runs into a defender who has legally *established his position* (has his feet firmly planted) instead of going around him or stopping his dribble. The defender must establish position before the offensive player's head and shoulder get past him. If the defender is moving when contact is made, he is called for illegal blocking, so defenders try to quickly get into position to *draw the charge* against the ball handler. Frequently, an official's judgment is all that separates a charge from an illegal blocking call.

- *Elbow Foul* — an elbow thrown by one player that makes contact with an opponent. That player is automatically ejected if the contact is made above the shoulder level, or even if below the shoulder level at the officials' discretion. An elbow thrown without contact is a violation and can be assessed a technical foul.

- *Fighting* — particularly discouraged in college where ejections and suspensions from future games result from the first such act; suspension for the entire season including tournament play is the penalty for a second offense. In the NBA, players are ejected, suspended and monetary fines levied.

- *Flagrant Foul* — when any foul committed (against any player, with or without the ball) is of such an unnecessary or excessive nature that injury could have resulted, such as punching and fighting. If the behavior is deemed unsporting, a player must be ejected. Its penalty is even harsher than a normal foul — not only does the wronged team get 2 free-throws, but it also gets possession on a throw-in after the free-throws.

- *Handchecking* — a defensive player cannot maintain hand contact with an offensive player in the defender's "sights" (facing him so he can see the offensive player's eyes).

- *Loose Ball Foul* — illegal contact that occurs while neither team is in possession of a live ball. The fouled team takes a throw-in, while the player who committed the foul and his team are credited with a foul.

- *Player-control foul* — (college only) when a foul is committed by the ball handler, no free-throws are awarded but the foul is still counted toward the player's personal and team fouls tally.

- *Punching* — even if no contact is made, this leads to the automatic ejection of the player or non-player who threw it.

- *Pushing* or *Holding* — a foul on a defensive player approaching the ball handler from the rear or on an offensive player guilty of pushing off of a defender in his approach to the basket for a shot. Grabbing a player's uniform to interfere with his movement is also illegal.

- *Screen, Illegal* — when an offensive player sets up a *screen* and is moving into his legal position, he must give the defensive player enough time to change direction and avoid a collision. An offensive player cannot sneak up behind an unsuspecting defender or take any position so close to a moving opponent that contact is inevitable (about 1 or 2 strides depending on the moving player's speed).

TECHNICAL FOULS

Technical fouls (also referred to as *Ts*) are called for behavior officials feel violate fair play. Players can be cited for any unsporting conduct, breach of etiquette or dirty play (such as taunting or "trash talking", using obscenities or fouling an opponent after a ball is clearly whistled dead), and fighting (where participants are also subject to immediate ejection). Any disrespect toward officials, even without vulgarity, can result in a technical, and players are never permitted to touch an official. Even tirades and continuous griping are not tolerated. Any excessive misconduct can lead to a player's ejection.

A technical foul awards a free-throw opportunity to the wronged team. In the NBA, 1 free-throw is awarded for every technical and the ball is then given to the team that had possession at the time the foul was called. In the case of *double technicals* simultaneously called on 2 players from opposing teams, no free-throws are taken. In college games the consequences of a technical are more serious, as 2 shots are awarded and the ball is given at midcourt to the non-offending team. For double technicals, both teams take two shots and the ball is given to the team the possession arrow designates.

When the technical is assessed, any player on the floor may take the free-throw, so teams generally choose their best free-throw shooter. Since the ball is awarded to a particular team after a technical free-throw, there is no need for either team to try to *rebound* a missed shot, so players do not line up along the foul lane as in a typical free-throw. In fact, in college they must all stand in the area beyond the *3-point line* and behind the *free-throw line extended*.

Misconduct by any non-players, such as coaches, is automatically called for a technical. So are some procedural fouls (such as changing the *starting lineup* once submitted, having too many players on the court, calling too many timeouts or for the second offense of *delaying the game*). Coaches and their personnel can also be called for a T if they step outside the boundary lines of the *coach's box*. They can leave this area only with an official's permission, to help break up a fight (head coach only), or to talk with the *scorer* or *timer*.

It is not unusual for a coach to get a technical; sometimes this is a tactic intentionally used by the coach to fire up his players. However, as with players, when 2 technicals (3 in college) are called against a coach, he is ejected from the remainder of the game and must remain in his team's dressing room or leave the building. In college, any technicals called against anyone on the team are counted against the head coach personally.

Illegal Defense
One team violation punished by a technical foul is *illegal defense*. This is a defensive team's attempt to use a *zone defense*, illegal in the NBA. It can only be called when the offense is in its frontcourt with the ball. The rules defining acceptable defensive coverage are quite complicated, establishing limits on how far away a defender can stand from an offensive player, and dividing the frontcourt into lower, middle and upper defensive areas. The easiest illegal defense for an untrained spectator to recognize is a defensive player standing alone in an area without guarding an opponent. This is often a player who gets caught in "no man's land," moving from assisting one teammate with a *double team* to assisting another teammate with a double team when the ball is passed. (See circled

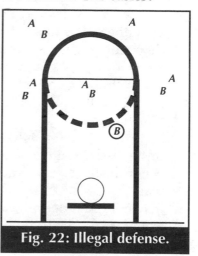

Fig. 22: Illegal defense.

defensive player in **Fig. 22**)

The first occurrence of this violation is a warning and provides the offense with a new 24-second clock and a throw-in from the free-throw line extended. After that, every subsequent occurrence is a technical foul against the defense. Any such violation during the last 24 seconds of any period (including overtime) is a technical foul, even if it is the first such occurrence of the game.

AWAY FROM THE PLAY
An away-from-the-play foul is a foul committed by a defender before the offense releases a throw-in or on any player without the ball (away from the play) in the final 2 minutes of a period (including overtime). The fouled team is awarded one free-throw (2 if it is an elbow or flagrant personal foul) and it also takes the ball out of bounds for a throw-in. This foul is often committed by a losing team deliberately trying to foul a player in the last few minutes in a desperate attempt to regain possession and score.

DOUBLE FOULS
Double fouls, where 2 opponents commit personal or technical fouls against each other at the same time, cancel each other out and no free-throws are taken. While they are counted toward a player's foul total, they are not added to the team fouls. The next step depends on what was happening when the fouls were called:
- if one team was in possession of the ball when the double foul was called, it takes the ball out of bounds for a throw-in and the 24-second clock is reset
- if neither team was in possession or if the fouls occurred while the ball was in mid-air on an unsuccessful field goal attempt, then a jump ball between any 2 opponents on the floor is used to restart play
- if a field goal attempt was successful, the team scored against takes the throw-in to continue the game

- if the double foul is the result of a difference in opinion by the officials, a jump ball at the center circle resumes the action

With the last few chapters in mind, you are ready to explore the **THINGS TO WATCH DURING PLAY / STRATEGY**.

THINGS TO LOOK FOR DURING PLAY / STRATEGY

To those spectators who simply watch the ball in a basketball game, it may seem that successful *field goals* are just a matter of good luck, and *fouls* called against a team just a matter of bad luck. In truth, scoring is achieved through a series of well-orchestrated moves between teammates in the face of close scrutiny by defenders who try to stop them. And although fouls are usually committed by accident, they are often the result of good deceptive moves on the part of the fouled player. Learning how to spot plays takes practice, but it can greatly increase your enjoyment in watching the game.

MATCH-UPS
A *match-up* is defined as any pairing of players on opposing teams who *guard* each other during a game. These pairings are vital as coaches try to exploit each opponent's known weaknesses when there are *mismatches* (a smaller or slower player against a bigger or faster one). Coaches try to avoid being on the short end of a mismatch, assigning players to guard opponents with similar abilities. As one team makes *substitutions*, the other needs to adjust its match-ups.

WHERE TO LOOK
First rid yourself of bad habits: do not just concentrate on the ball. Instead, try to absorb all 10 players on the court and allow yourself to find patterns. Keep in mind the court is divided into 3 invisible *lanes*, the middle area where the *key* is and 2 *wing lanes* along the sides of the court. The offense generally looks to move toward the *open lane* (the one with the least number of players). This forces the defense to spread out, making its job more difficult.

Look for the number of players moving on the court. If there are 1 or 2 players in the *post* standing still, they will become the hub of the activity as their teammates move around them. Remember to watch the *ball handler* (not just the ball) even <u>after</u> he has passed the ball to figure out if he is setting himself up to get it back again.

HALF-COURT OFFENSE

The opposite of the fast break, where a team takes the time to develop a play in its *frontcourt*, is called the *half-court offense* or *set offense*. The next few sections give examples of plays a team tries in this type of offense.

The Give-and-Go

One of the most basic plays on offense, the *give-and-go*, occurs when one player (a giver or passer) passes the ball to a teammate (a *receiver*), *cuts* to the basket and then gets the ball back as soon as he is *open*. What make this sequence successful is that the defender who was guarding the giver relaxes slightly when the ball is passed to another player. As soon as he slackens his defense, the giver is able to get open to get the ball back and *drive* to the basket or shoot.

Screening Plays

A *screening play* is any play where one offensive player (the *screener*) gives his teammate room by standing between him and a defender. (See **Fig. 23**) This *screen* (or *pick*) often gives the teammate a chance to take an open shot with no defender in his face. The most effective screens are set by big players such as *forwards* and *centers* to free up their smaller teammates from defenders. While watching play, any time you see an offensive player just standing in the middle of the frontcourt with his hands to his sides not even looking for the ball, he is probably looking to set up a screen. There are several types of screening plays you should learn to recognize:

Pinch-Post — similar to the give-and-go, except the giver passes to an open teammate in the post who acts as the screener. The giver then *fakes* to one side but cuts to other side close to the screener, preventing his defender from

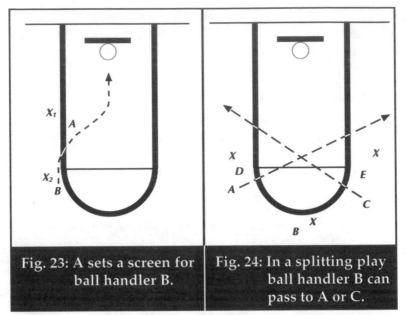

| Fig. 23: A sets a screen for ball handler B. | Fig. 24: In a splitting play ball handler B can pass to A or C. |

staying with him. This defender has been *picked off* by the giver who is open to get the ball back from the screener and shoot it.

Backdoor — this is a 3-player variation of the give-and-go where a player who was not the original giver is the one who gets open and is given the ball to shoot instead. When the defenders all concentrate on the pass to the *post* they often ignore a player behind them on the wing who is open to then receive the pass from the post, and go in for a *layup*.

Pick-and-roll or *Screen-and-roll* — after screening an opponent to get a teammate free, the screener rolls (or pivots) toward the basket to receive a pass from the ball handler and shoot. The shot will usually be a layup.

SPLITTING
Splitting is a 3-person play where 2 players (called *cutters*) crisscross as they cut past the post to give a ball handler the option of passing the ball to either one. (See **Fig. 24**) These splitting plays are usually aided by screens:

Double Screen — this splitting pattern has the passer and one of the cutters stop at the post to provide a *double screen* for the other cutter. These are particularly helpful to *perimeter* shooters or if one of the screeners is able to get free and roll to the basket.

Stack — 2 big teammates standing in the *low post* on the same side of the *3-second* area set screens for each other or a double screen for a teammate. Usually this pattern uses a screen by the center to get a forward free.

ONE-ON-ONE PLAYS
Sometimes 4 offensive players will clear a path for a *1-on-1* showdown between their most talented player and a defender (also called a *clear out*). These 4 teammates set up a stack on both sides of the middle lane while the 1-on-1 moves to the top of the key. In this position they are available to receive a pass if the defense *double teams* their ball handler.

AWAY FROM THE PLAY
After you identify one of the basic offensive plays in basketball described above, look to see what the other players are doing — what is going on away from the ball will tell more of the story. These other players may be
- standing still and observing
- moving into defensive position for a transition
- preparing for an alternative offensive play
- positioning themselves for a rebound
- positioning themselves for a pass

It is important to pay attention to how well a team sets screens on the *weakside* (the side away from the ball) and how the defense is responding, because this is often where the next play develops. In a game as rapid as basketball, the spectator needs to stay a few steps ahead — you can follow the action better if you identify several possible upcoming plays.

FAST BREAK

The *fast break* (or the *run and shoot*) is one of the most exciting plays to watch and one of the easiest ways for a smaller, quicker team to score. Generally, this play begins when a player grabs a missed shot at one end (*defensive rebound*) and immediately sends an *outlet pass* toward *midcourt* where most of his teammates are waiting. These teammates can sprint to reach their basket and quickly shoot before enough of their opponents catch up to stop them. By outnumbering the defense, this pattern provides an easy opportunity to score or to get *offensive rebounds* in case the shot is missed.

Here are some patterns you might see, where the first digit of the notation represents the number of players on offense during the fast break and the second digit represents the number of players on defense:

3-on-2 break — the most common variety, where 2 offensive players run down the two wing lanes a few feet ahead of the ball handler who runs down the middle lane. (In addition, a few feet behind and to one side of the ball handler is the trailer who is ready to take a *jump shot* off a *blind pass*. The fifth offensive player is the rebounder who initiated the fast break who waits back in defensive position prepared for a quick *transition*.) Since there are only 2 defenders, one of the 3 offensive players will remain open when the defenders commit themselves to guarding 2 of them, and the ball handler needs to make a quick decision — to pass to an open teammate or take the ball to the basket himself.

2-on-1 break — the goal of the offense here is to make the lone defender commit to guarding one player so the ball handler can decide to go in himself for a layup or pass to his teammate. The longer a defender waits to commit, the more he forces the ball handler to go all the way to the basket himself.

3-on-1 break — this provides a huge advantage for the offense because 2 of its players are unguarded and can pass freely among themselves, almost always resulting in a score. However, the defender's teammates are ready to greatly outnumber the opponent for any play at the other end.

FULL COURT PRESS

When several defenders start to pressure the offense in the *backcourt*, it is called a *full-court press*. The press can disrupt some teams by hindering them from bringing the ball into the frontcourt and causing *turnovers* near the opponent's basket.

Fig. 25: Double team.

TYPES OF DEFENSES
Man-to-Man Defense
In the *man-to-man defense* each player on the defending team is responsible for guarding a particular player on the opposing team. When 2 defenders join forces to guard against a single offensive player, it is called a *double team* (See **Fig. 25**). In this type of defense, a defender sometimes *picks up* his player as soon as the ball is brought *inbounds* in the backcourt in an attempt to cause a *10-second violation* or turnover closer to the defender's own basket.

Zone Defense
In a *zone defense*, each defender is responsible for an area of the court, and he must guard any player who ventures into that area. Usually, as soon as the ball enters a zone, the defender of that area will get some assistance from one or more of his teammates. The zone defense is used extensively at the college level, but is not permitted in the *NBA* because the league tries to promote one-on-one match-ups which are more exciting.

There are 3 general types of zone defenses: the 3-2, the 1-3-1 and the 2-3. (See **Fig. 26**) The numbers describe the position of the defenders as seen by the offense from midcourt. Which defense a team employs will depend on the relative strengths and weaknesses of their players and those of their opponents:

3-2 zone — 3 defenders are positioned across the court in front of the *foul circle* with 2 on the outer sides of the *foul lane*. Considered an offensive zone, it prepares a team to make a quick transition to a fast break with more players close to their basket.

2-3 zone — this is more of a defensive zone that sets up 3 players near the basket to prevent the offense from getting a close shot or a layup. This is the defense preferred by teams with taller, slower players who are less likely to fast break.

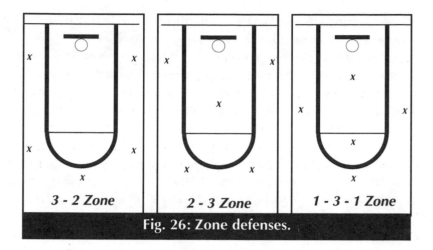

| 3 - 2 Zone | 2 - 3 Zone | 1 - 3 - 1 Zone |

Fig. 26: Zone defenses.

1-3-1 zone— also a defensive zone which sets up 1 player outside each foul lane and 3 players in a line from the foul line to below the basket who will fall back to form a tight triangle below the basket as the offense advances. This is the defense sometimes used when the offensive team has at least one player who is good at shooting or passing from the top of the key because it places a defender there while the 3-2 and 2-3 defenses do not.

Man-to-Man vs. Zone
The man-to-man defense gives offensive players less room to shoot from the *outside* (or *perimeter*) than the zone because each player is guarded by a defender specifically assigned to him, whereas zone defenders merely cover an area. However, zone defenses are better able to stop a dominant offensive player from scoring *inside* because defenders provide help to overmatched teammates in nearby zones.

THREE-POINT SHOOTING
Three-point shots ignite the fans and boost a team's morale. They can change a game very quickly—even a 9 point deficit can be erased by just 3 baskets when a team has good 3-point shooters. Teams like to put their best shooters on the floor whenever they are way behind with

time running out, so look for substitutions to insert these shooters and watch them try to get open for 3-point opportunities. A team with great 3-point shooters does more than just score points in big chunks, though. It also forces the defense to guard them more closely away from the basket, drawing defenders away from its inside players to make it easier for them to score.

In college, a player fouled in the act of shooting behind the *3-point line* will go to the foul line for 3 *free-throw* opportunities — which is only fair since he was prevented from getting 3 points. In the NBA, however, a player going for 3 who is fouled only gets 2 free-throws. On rare occasion, this creates an incentive for opponents to foul good 3-point shooters behind the 3-point line — risking 2 points *on the line* instead of 3 from the field.

TIMEOUTS

While they are precious and usually saved for the most critical moments, *timeouts* can be used by a team in a number of strategic ways:

- to stop its opponent's momentum when it is on a *run*
- since a timeout allows the offense to inbound the ball at midcourt instead of way back in the backcourt after the timeout, a team uses it when it needs to save precious seconds and avoid the potential for a *10-second violation*
- in the final minutes of a close game, a team ready for a *throw-in* may use up a timeout just to change its play in response to how it observed the defense setting up for the next play
- if the defense is particularly tight on any throw-in and the thrower is unable to get the ball inbounds within the allotted 5 seconds, he may call a timeout rather than commit the violation and lose *possession*
- at any point during play that a player feels he is about to commit a turnover, he may call for a timeout and receive a temporary reprieve as his team caucuses on the *sidelines*

END OF PERIOD STRATEGIES
Playing the Clock
Teams who are leading near the end of a game can employ a series of time-related strategies to slow the pace down. The logic is that the longer a team holds the ball, the fewer opportunities its opponents will have to catch up. In playing the clock, a team waits until most of the *shot clock* has expired before shooting and then takes only high percentage shots. To pass the time, it moves slowly with the ball, dribbling or passing frequently around the perimeter. Near the end of a close game, these delay tactics inspire opponents to purposely commit fouls since the clock stops during free-throws and they get possession after the attempts.

Intentional Fouling and Free-Throws
When intentionally fouling an opponent to stop the clock, a team clearly wants to foul the player with the least likelihood of completing his free-throw attempt — one with a low *free-throw percentage* (65% or less). However, the defense must be careful not to commit a *flagrant foul*, which would also give the fouled team possession after the free-throws. The team that knows it is going to get fouled tries to keep the ball in the hands of its player with the best free-throw percentage (80% or higher). Since time is running out, the defense usually cannot wait until the ball is in the right player's hands to commit the foul, giving the offense the advantage.

Now that you are on your way to identifying plays and strategies, it is time to introduce you to the structure of professional basketball in the U.S. Let us examine the **NBA TEAMS, DIVISIONS & CONFERENCES.**

NBA TEAMS, DIVISIONS & CONFERENCES

As of the 1994-95 season, the *National Basketball Association* (*NBA*) had 27 teams divided into 4 *divisions* and 2 *conferences*. The names of these divisions and conferences generally reflect the geographic regions represented by the teams. Until the 1995-96 season when 2 more teams join the NBA, the teams will continue to be split as follows:

Eastern Conference:
- Atlantic Division (7 teams)
- Central Division (7 teams)

Western Conference:
- Pacific Division (7 teams)
- Midwest Division (6 teams)

An example of how the actual NBA teams are listed in the newspaper is located in the chapter **DECIPHERING BASKETBALL STATISTICS IN THE NEWSPAPER**.

THE BIRTH OF THE NBA
The precursors to the NBA were the *Basketball Association of America* (*BAA*) and the *National Basketball League* (*NBL*). All 3 leagues changed their size many times over the years through *expansion* that came from the creation of new teams, the addition of existing teams from outside the league and by mergers with other leagues.

The NBL was formed in 1937, and though its progress was sidetracked by World War II, it continued to add *franchises* through the late 1940s. The BAA was started at the end of the war by operators of large National Hockey League arenas who wanted to make greater use of their facilities and capitalize on the growing popularity of basketball. Only 3 of the original 11 teams that began its first season in 1946 remain in the NBA today — the *Boston Celtics*, New York Knickerbockers and Philadelphia Warriors (who later moved to San Francisco).

Though the Baltimore Bullets joined the BAA in 1947-48, it was not until 1948-49, when the 4 best teams of the rival NBL (Fort Wayne Pistons, Indianapolis Jets, Minneapolis Lakers and Rochester Royals) joined the BAA's Western Division, that the league experienced its first official expansion.

The NBA finally came into existence as the last 6 NBL teams were absorbed into the BAA in 1949-50, and the entire league with its 17 teams and 3 divisions was renamed. Its teams were:

Eastern Division:	Central Division:	Western Division:
Baltimore Bullets*	Chicago Stags	Anderson Packers
Boston Celtics*	Fort Wayne Pistons*	Denver Nuggets
NY Knickerbockers*	Minnepolis Lakers*	Indianapolis Olympians*
Philadelphia Warriors*	Rochester Royals*	Sheboygen (Wis) Redskins
Syracuse Nationals*	St. Louis Bombers	Tri-Cities Blackhawks*
Washington Capitols*		Waterloo (Iowa) Hawks

By the 1950-51 season only 11 teams remained (* above) and in subsequent seasons the league stabilized at 8 teams. The league did not grow again until 10 years later when the Chicago Packers (who later became the Baltimore/ Washington Bullets) joined in 1961, followed by the Chicago Bulls in 1966. Two more franchises were added the next year (Seattle Supersonics and San Diego/Houston Rockets), and 2 more the year after that (Phoenix Suns and Milwaukee Bucks).

THE ABA MERGER

Meanwhile, the *American Basketball Association* (*ABA*) came into existence in 1967 with 11 teams, to which it added 2 more in 1968. Financial woes plagued the new league so it was not long before the ABA began contemplating a merger with the NBA. By 1970, the NBA had expanded to 17 teams and split into the 4 divisions and 2 conferences which remain in existence today. The NBA's 18th team, the New Orleans Jazz, joined the Central Division in 1974.

The merger with the ABA finally took place in 1976, adding the Denver Nuggets, Indiana Pacers, New York (later New Jersey) Nets and San Antonio Spurs, requiring a major realignment of the now 22 NBA teams. A few more relocations (Los Angeles Clippers, Sacramento Kings and Utah Jazz) and one expansion (Dallas Mavericks in 1980) marked the early 1980s.

RECENT EXPANSION

The late 1980s brought aggressive expansion by the NBA as it introduced 4 new teams in 2 years:

Charlotte Hornets (1988)   Miami Heat (1988)
Minnesota Timberwolves (1989)   Orlando Magic (1989)

Beginning in 1995, the NBA's expansion efforts will move outside the United States for the first time, as 2 Canadian teams will be added in Toronto and Vancouver.

LIST OF CURRENT NBA TEAMS

Table 2 is an alphabetized list of NBA teams, the year they joined the league, and their division and conference:

TABLE 2: CURRENT NBA TEAMS

Team	Year	Division	Conference
Atlanta Hawks[1]	1949	Central	Eastern
Boston Celtics	1946	Atlantic	Eastern
Charlotte Hornets	1988	Central	Eastern
Chicago Bulls	1966	Central	Eastern
Cleveland Cavaliers	1970	Central	Eastern
Dallas Mavericks	1980	Midwest	Western
Denver Nuggets	1976	Midwest	Western
Detroit Pistons[2]	1948	Central	Eastern
Golden State Warriors[3]	1946	Pacific	Western
Houston Rockets[4]	1967	Midwest	Western
Indiana Pacers	1976	Central	Eastern
Los Angeles Clippers[5]	1970	Pacific	Western
Los Angeles Lakers[6]	1948	Pacific	Western
Miami Heat	1988	Atlantic	Eastern
Milwaukee Bucks	1968	Central	Eastern
Minnesota Timberwolves[7]	1989	Midwest	Western
New Jersey Nets[8]	1976	Atlantic	Eastern
NY Knickerbockers[9]	1946	Atlantic	Eastern
Orlando Magic	1989	Atlantic	Eastern
Philadelphia 76ers[10]	1963	Atlantic	Eastern
Phoenix Suns	1968	Pacific	Western
Portland Trailblazers	1970	Pacific	Western
Sacramento Kings[11]	1948	Pacific	Western
San Antonio Spurs	1976	Midwest	Western
Seattle Sonics[12]	1967	Pacific	Western
Toronto Raptors[13]	1995	—	—
Utah Jazz[14]	1974	Midwest	Western
Vancouver Grizzlies[13]	1995	—	—
Washington Bullets[15]	1961	Atlantic	Eastern

[1] Tri-Cities Blackhawks '49-'51; Milwaukee Hawks '51-'55, St. Louis Hawks '55-'68
[2] Fort Wayne Pistons '48-'57
[3] Philadelphia Warriors '46-'62; San Francisco Warriors '62-'71
[4] San Diego Rockets '67-'71
[5] Buffalo Braves '70-'78; San Diego Clippers '78-'84
[6] Minneapolis Lakers '48-'60
[7] This team considered for relocation to New Orleans for the 1994-95 season but the NBA (Steering) Committee denied the move; at press time a group of Minnesota investors were bidding to keep the team in their city which is the NBA's preference
[8] New York Nets '76-'77
[9] More commonly called the New York Knicks
[10] Syracuse Nationals '49-'63
[11] Rochester Royals '48-'57; Cincinnati Royals '57-'72; Kansas City-Omaha Kings '72-'75; Kansas City Kings '75-'85
[12] Requested and was granted name change from Seattle Supersonics for 1994-95 season
[13] The NBA has not yet determined whether the divisions and conferences will be realigned for the 1995 expansion teams
[14] New Orleans Jazz '74-'80
[15] Chicago Packers '61-'62; Chicago Zephyrs "62-'63; Baltimore Bullets '63-'73, Capital Bullets '73-'74

NBA SEASON & PLAYOFFS

REGULAR SEASON
The *NBA* begins its 82-game *regular season* the first Friday in November, ending the 3rd Sunday in April. Since a season overlaps 2 calendar years, it is referred to by both (e.g., the 1994-95 season). A team usually plays half of its games at home and half on the road. Teams within a single conference will meet most often, playing against each other a minimum of 4 times during the season and creating intense regional rivalries. Yet NBA teams also play every team in the league (including teams in the other conference) twice — once at home and once on the road — to promote national rivalries as well. Since 1990, NBA teams have also played several of these games abroad each season.

During regular-season play, the 27 NBA teams compete for the top spots in the *standings*. Teams are ranked within each *division* based on a simple *win-loss* or *winning percentage* (no game ever ends in a *tie* in the NBA). The team with the best *record* (the highest winning percentage) is the *division leader*. More on standings is discussed in the next chapter on **DECIPHERING STATISTICS IN THE NEWSPAPER**.

PLAYOFFS
After the regular-season schedule of games is over, the 16 teams with the best overall records advance to the *post-season*, otherwise known as the *NBA Playoffs*. The dates for the playoffs vary each year depending on how long each *round* lasts, but generally they begin in late April and last until mid-June. As the regular-season draws to a close, teams *clinch* playoff spots as soon as their records assure they will be in the top 16.

The top 8 teams in each of the 2 conferences advance to the playoffs. There are 4 rounds used to narrow the number of teams by eliminating the losers of each. Teams are paired up to play a *best-of-seven series* in each of the rounds, except the *first round* which is decided by a *best-of-five series*. A best-of-seven series means the first team to win 4 games emerges victorious. This can be done in as few as 4, 5 or 6 games — although the more evenly matched 2 teams are, the more likely a series will go the full 7 games. In a best-of-five series, the first to win 3 games advances (it can be done in 3, 4 or 5 games).

Over a 7-game series it is less likely that a weaker team will get lucky and advance to the next round than if only a single game was played. However, *upsets* are more likely in the first round, since fewer (only 5) games are played, as evidenced by some surprises in recent years.

The 16 playoff teams are *seeded* #1 - #8 within each of the 2 conferences. The 8 teams within each conference play each other in 4 head-to-head series. Within each conference, the division leader with the best record is seeded #1. The other division leader is seeded number #2, even if this team's record is not the second best in the entire conference. The teams with the next 6 best records from any division are seeded #3 through #8. For this reason, one division may be represented by more teams than the other.

In the first round, the #1 team in each conference plays against the #8 in the conference, #2 vs. #7, #3 vs. #6, and #4 vs. #5. (See **Fig. 27**) The 4 winners within each conference play each other in the second round, also called the *conference semifinals*. Two teams advance to each *conference final* (or third round), where the winner is crowned conference champion.

These 2 conference champions meet in the fourth, or final round, called the *NBA Finals*, to determine the best team in the league. The winner is permanently awarded the *Larry*

O'Brien Trophy. Although there can be a new champion every year, some teams have established dynasties, reclaiming the trophy several years in succession. For more on this, see the chapter on **GREAT TEAMS & DYNASTIES**.

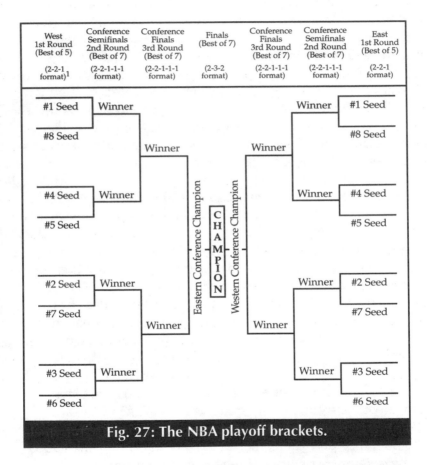

Fig. 27: The NBA playoff brackets.

[1] The number of games played at one site before changing sites; each series begins with 2 home games for the team seeded higher (or with the best record).

NBA ALL-STAR GAME & TEAMS

ALL-STAR GAME

The idea of holding a mid-season game featuring the best players from different *NBA* teams was born in 1951. The first *All-Star Game* was nearly canceled though, as most people, including the league's *Commissioner Maurice Podoloff*, thought it would flop. It was only at the insistence of the indomitable Walter Brown (then-owner of the *Boston Celtics*) who took over responsibility for its expenses and potential losses, that the game was held.

Today, it is one of the most exciting events in sports. Beginning in 1984, its format was expanded into an entire All-Star Weekend held every mid-season (usually in February). The festivities include a Legends game, a series of contests from slam dunking to long distance shooting, and educational programming for kids preceding the Sunday All-Star Game. The location is changed every year.

Fans submit ballots (found at league games or in local newspapers) to select the top 5 players on each of the 2 teams, East and West. The player at each position (*guard, forward* and *center*) with the most votes automatically starts the game for his conference. Each All-Star team is led by the coach of the NBA team with the best record in that conference on the balloting deadline date, accompanied by the assistant coaches he regularly works with. It is the league's coaches who select 7 additional *reserves* per team to round out the *roster* and create a *bench*.

The All-Star Game is unique in that every player on each team will see some playing time — after all, it is a spectacle for the pleasure of the fans. Since the emphasis is on exciting offensive plays, the scores of these contests are much higher than those of most regular NBA games. A definite rivalry divides the nation, although through 1994, the East had won 28 games to the West's 16 victories.

ALL-NBA TEAMS

The teams that play at the All-Star Game should not be confused with the *All-NBA Teams*. Players on the All-NBA Team are selected at the conclusion of the regular season by basketball broadcasters and writers because they excelled at playing their particular position during the season. They do not play a game together. Today, there is a First Team, a Second Team and (since 1988-89) a Third Team, so 3 players at each position are honored. Since 1962, there has also been a 5-member *NBA All-Rookie Team*, selected by the league's coaches, to honor the top rookie at each position, and since 1968, *NBA All-Defensive Teams* (First and Second) have also been selected by the coaches.

THE NBA LOTTERY, DRAFT, TRADES, FREE AGENCY & LABOR ISSUES

THE NBA DRAFT & LOTTERY

The *NBA* teams select, or *draft*, new team members from among a pool of candidates, most of whom are recent college graduates or talented foreign players. Occasionally, talented and hopeful underclassmen test their chances by leaving school early — a scenario likely to become more common with the passage of a recent *NCAA* rule permitting such players to return to college if they are disappointed with how they fare in the draft. Today, the lottery is held during the *halftime* break of a *playoff* game — usually in late May — about 1 month before the actual draft takes place in late June.

One purpose of the draft is to maintain balanced competition throughout the league by affording those teams with the worst *win-loss records* the opportunity to obtain the best available talent first and thereby improve in subsequent years. Sometimes a team will select the best player at a position that team needs to fill on its *roster*. Each selection is made during a *round* (where each team gets a turn to make a pick). Although the NBA held its first college draft prior to the start of the 1947-48 season, the idea of using rounds was not introduced until 1957. In past years there have been as many as 21 rounds, but today there are only 2 rounds in each draft.

To assure that teams did not purposely lose (throw) their final games to get a top draft pick, teams used a simple coin flip to determine the selection sequence up through 1984. Beginning in June 1985, the *NBA* Board of Governors adopted a *lottery* system for non-*playoff* teams to determine the order of selection in the *first round* of the NBA *draft*. In all succeeding rounds, teams picked in the inverse order of their win-loss records. The lottery was later modified to guarantee that the last team in the NBA would, in the worse case, receive the 4th pick in the draft.

The draft was altered yet again in 1990, for the then 11 non-playoff teams, to provide a weighted system that gave the team with the worst record the greatest chance of obtaining the number 1 pick (#11 had 11 numbered ping-pong balls in a drum, #10 had 10 balls, #2 had 2 balls, etc). This served the NBA well through 1993, when the Orlando Magic defied statistical probability and obtained the number 1 pick for the second consecutive year, despite having the best overall record among non-playoff teams (a 1 out of 66 — or 1.5% — chance of occurrence).

The "Orlando repeat incident" prompted the NBA to revamp its lottery yet again. The new system uses 14 balls numbered 1-14. The procedure involves drawing 4 balls to create one of 1,001 4-number combinations (14x13x12x11/4x3x2x1). The team with the worst record is assigned 250 of these 1,001 combinations for a 25% chance of obtaining the number 1 pick. The team with the second worst record gets 203 (or a 20.3% chance), etc. This new system also drastically reduces the likelihood of a team with the best record among non-playoff contenders (like Orlando in 1993) getting the number 1 pick from 1.5% to 0.5%.

EXPANSION & OTHER DRAFTS
Whenever the NBA adds teams through *expansion* (1966, 1968, 1970, 1974, 1980, 1988, 1989 and 1995), a separate *expansion draft* is held where each existing team is permitted to protect a number of its most important players, leaving the others available for selection by the expansion team(s). A number of other drafts have been held over the last 2 decades, including the 1971 Hardship Drafts (following a lawsuit requiring the NBA and *ABA* to include underclassmen in their drafts), the 1972 and 1976 ABA Dispersal Drafts (to absorb players from dissolved

ABA teams into the NBA), and the 1973 ABA Special Circumstances Draft.

SALARY CAP & FREE AGENCY
Even though a player is drafted by a team, he must still negotiate a contract. The NBA has tried to prevent having players' salaries spiral out of control by establishing a *salary cap* — limiting the dollar amount a team can pay all of its players collectively in a season. Players can sign a variety of contracts up to several years in length. At the expiration of this contract, a player becomes a *free agent*. At that point, his team can re-negotiate with him, or another team can make an offer. However, the player's original team is given the option to make a counteroffer within 15 days if the player is a *restricted free agent*. A team does not have this right of first refusal if the player is an *unrestricted free agent*.

TRADES
Teams are allowed to trade players on their rosters, players who have been drafted and draft choices. These trades include the players or the rights to future draft picks (or both) as incentives. Since the NBA has established a *trading deadline* (the 16th Thursday of the season which usually falls in February) this is an important time to watch for a flurry of trading activity. After this date, no players can be traded for the remainder of that season.

LABOR NEGOTIATIONS
The NBA's *collective bargaining agreement* with its players expired in July 1994, and both sides are spending time at the negotiating table and in court. The *Players' Association* wants no salary cap, no draft, total unrestricted free agency and for players to have a say before they are traded. The owners not only want the draft and the salary cap to stay, but they would like to see a rookie salary cap added to avoid huge first year contracts. The first battle was won by the owners when a court held the draft and salary cap were both legal. Stay tuned, as this is far from over.

THE NCAA & THE FINAL FOUR

THE NCAA

The *National Collegiate Athletic Association* (*NCAA*)is a voluntary association comprised of over 1000 colleges, universities and related organizations in the U.S., from large state institutions to small, privately funded colleges. The role of the NCAA is to protect the integrity of amateurism for student-athletes, and assist these educational institutions in establishing standards and determining the proper role of athletics within their programs. A number of committees develop the NCAA's overall policies and procedures, and the specific rules for each of the 21 sports it administers.

The NCAA enforces the rules and regulations the colleges vote to impose upon themselves. In recent years the NCAA has taken an aggressive view toward violations of these rules and standards, and has meted out punishments that include monetary fines and suspension from tournament participation for several years. The NCAA has the power to limit the playing time of a particular athlete or can even prevent a school from televising its games, thereby affecting an individual's career potential or the college's recruiting ability in the future. It also imposes a variety of educational requirements designed to prepare athletes for the real world (since the average *NBA* career — for the few who make it — is only 3.5 years). Many colleges have clubs of alumni supporting certain sports who call themselves *boosters*, but they are unrelated to the NCAA.

COLLEGE TEAMS & CONFERENCES

In basketball, the colleges themselves are divided into 3 divisions, based on their competitive level: Divisions I, II and III, with I being the best. Only Divisions I and II offer athletic scholarships. The schools are further divided into conferences. Listed below are the various conferences (those marked with an * are better-known and usually represented by more than one team each year):

Atlantic Coast (ACC)*	Metro Atlantic	Southeastern*
Atlantic 10*	Mid-American	(East & West)
Big East*	Mid-Continent	Southern
Big Eight*	Mid-Eastern Athletic	Southland
Big Sky	Midwestern Collegiate	Southwest
Big South	Missouri Valley	Southwestern Athletic
Big Ten*	North Atlantic	Sun Belt
Big West	Northeast	Trans-America
Colonial Athletic	Ohio Valley	West Coast
Great Midwest*	Pacific-10 (Pac 10)*	Western Athletic
Ivy League	Patriot	

Each team plays a schedule of *regular-season* games from mid-November through March of the next year, mostly against the teams within the same conference (intraconference) and a handful against teams in other conferences (interconference). Only the intraconference games count toward determining each conference's champion. *Exhibition* games played prior to or during the season are not counted as part of a team's *record*.

THE NCAA TOURNAMENT & FINAL FOUR

The NCAA tournament has been in existence since 1939 when only 8 teams competed. Expansion of the *field* took place over time: 16 teams in 1951, 32 in 1975 and finally 64 in 1985. Until 1975, only one team per conference was represented. Today, a Selection Committee *seeds* the 30 *automatic bids* (teams that finished in 1st place in their conference) and 34 *at-large selections* (other teams chosen based on their records) (32 of each for the women's tournament). The teams that are selected, and sometimes more importantly who they will play and where (since some neutral sites are so close to a team's home that it is like having home court advantage) are decided behind closed doors over the weekend before the pairings are announced.

The seeding process is controversial, involving difficult decision-making by the committee. In the past, the

81

committee looked to the Associated Press (AP) and USA Today/CNN polls (ranking the top 25 college teams and released weekly on Mondays of the regular season) for assistance. However, in recent years greater parity among colleges produced many different teams that laid claim to the #1 ranking throughout the season, and has made the job of deciding which teams are truly better more difficult. Since the tournament is a single-elimination contest, seedings are very important — the higher a team is seeded, the easier its first round games are, and the more likely it is to advance.

The 64 teams actually battle it out in 4 regional groups of 16: West Regional, Midwest Regional, East Regional, Southeast Regional. (For the women's Tournament, the regions are the Mideast, Midwest, West and East.) Teams are seeded #1-#16 in each region, and #1 plays #16, #2 vs. #15, #3 vs. #14, etc. (See sample *brackets* in **Fig. 28**) The games take place at 8 neutral sites (some of which change each year) for the first round, which is followed by a second round, regional semifinals, regional finals, culminating in the Final Four, which brings together the champions of each region. The 2 winners of the Final Four Semifinals square off for the Championship on a Monday night, usually the first week of April. Since the entire tournament takes nearly 3 weeks during which it takes over the sports world, it has been dubbed *"March Madness."*

OFFICE POOLS
However difficult, the final decisions of the Selection Committee are revealed on the Sunday evening before the tournament commences in mid-March. The tournament begins at 9:00 am EST Thursday of the same week, so during the 3 days between the announcement of the pairings and the start of March Madness, offices and assorted groups of friends around the nation frantically place their picks in *pools*.

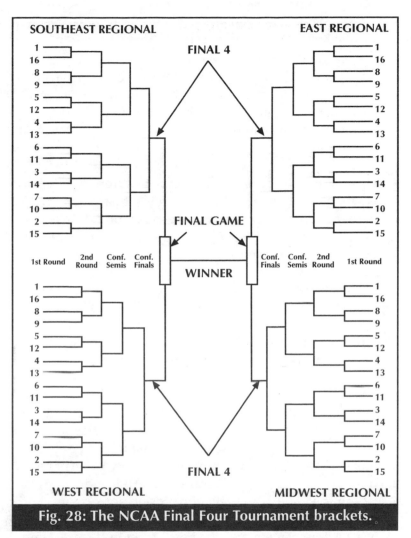

SOUTHEAST REGIONAL

1
16
8
9
5
12
4
13
6
11
3
14
7
10
2
15

FINAL 4

EAST REGIONAL

1
16
8
9
5
12
4
13
6
11
3
14
7
10
2
15

FINAL GAME

1st Round | 2nd Round | Conf. Semis | Conf. Finals

WINNER

Conf. Finals | Conf. Semis | 2nd Round | 1st Round

1
16
8
9
5
12
4
13
6
11
3
14
7
10
2
15

1
16
8
9
5
12
4
13
6
11
3
14
7
10
2
15

FINAL 4

WEST REGIONAL

MIDWEST REGIONAL

Fig. 28: The NCAA Final Four Tournament brackets.

To run a pool, 2 or more people compete on who can best guess the winners of the tournament. Fill in the name of each team you think will advance to the next round on the form provided in the newspaper when the pairings are announced. One person should run the pool and collect everyone's picks, keeping them posted at the end of each round on how they are faring. Here are some variations on how to calculate points (the winner accumulates the most) — though you can easily develop variations of your own:

- Simple Pool — receive one point for each correct choice.

- Increasing Points Pool — receive 1 point for each correct first round pick, 2 points for each correct second round pick, 3 for each correct regional semifinal pick, 4 for each correct regional final winner, 5 for each correct Final Four Semifinal winner and 6 points for the correct champion.

- Upset Pool — this pool can be the most fun — an *upset* is when a team seeded lower upsets a team seeded higher (e.g., #15 beats #2 in the First Round, and it does happen!). The points are calculated as in the Increasing Points pool, plus points are given for the seed differential of every upset. For example, if you correctly picked that #15 would beat #2 in the First Round, you get 1 point for a correct pick PLUS 13 points for the upset (15-2). This pool should also reward every correct Final Four pick with 5 bonus points to encourage participants to choose only realistic upsets.

NIT

The *National Invitational Tournament*, first held in 1938 when the Metropolitan Basketball Writers of New York sponsored it, is the oldest college postseason tournament. Today, the *NIT* takes place at the same time as the NCAA tournament, starting one day earlier and ending the Wednesday preceding the Final Four weekend at Madison Square Garden. The best Division I teams that were not selected to the NCAA tournament and the best Division II teams gain one of 32 *berths* to the NIT as selected by a committee (for both men and women). Today's rules prevent one team from winning both the NCAA and NIT tournaments, but in 1950 City College of New York (*CCNY*) accomplished the feat. The NIT also sponsors an unrelated pre-season invitational tournament in mid-November that showcases the 20 best college teams and kicks off the college season.

INDIVIDUAL & TEAM STATISTICS

Points (PTS): 2 are awarded for each *field goal*, 1 for each *free-throw* and 3 for every *3-point shot*.

Scoring Average or *Points-Per-Game* (*PPG*): total number of points scored by a player during the season divided by the number of games played. The top scorers average 30 points-per-game.

Field Goal Percentage (*FG%*): the number of successful field goals divided by the number of attempted field goals for a player or a team. An analysis is done every quarter for both teams — not surprisingly, the team with the lower percentage is usually behind. A team is shooting well if it has a FG% over 50%. Players who take inside shots can have a FG% as high as 60%, while most outside shooters make less than 50% of their shots.

Three-Point Field Goal Percentage (3-PT%): the same as the field goal percentage but calculated only for 3-point shots.

Free-Throw Percentage (FT%): the number of successful free-throws divided by the number of attempted free-throws for a player or team. It is important to a team looking to intentionally foul its opponent — it seeks out the player with the lowest percentage because he is more likely to miss the free-throws. An *NBA* team will have a FT% of around 75%, while college teams fare worse at the line, shooting around 65%. A good NBA player can complete 85% or more of his free-throw attempts.

Assists (A): credited to a player whose pass to a teammate directly leads to a field goal. The all-time best players average 13 in a game, while the record is 30.

Bench Scoring: a percentage or total number of points scored by players other than the *starting lineup*, which shows the offensive strength of a team's *bench*.

Defensive Rebounds (DR): the number of rebounds a player or team has on the defensive end of the court.

Offensive Rebounds (OR): the number of rebounds a player or team has on its offensive end of the court. These are far less common than defensive rebounds. A team with more of these is more aggressive and more likely to control the ball to score.

Total Rebounds (TR): OR plus DR for a player or team.

Steals: when a defensive player gets the ball away from an opponent who controls it. Since players are relatively adept at controlling the ball, steals are hard to get — the highest number in a single game was 11 while the highest average per game is less than 3.

Turnovers: the number of times a team loses *possession* of the ball without taking a shot or without having the other team steal the ball, usually as the result of a *floor violation* or a bad pass that goes *out of bounds*. The team with the higher total is more likely to lose the game and a good defense will cause the offense to commit more of these.

Blocked shots: a player with the ability to stop a field goal attempt can frustrate an offense. These are also rare, with the highest per game average between 3 and 4, although there were 17 by one player in a 1973 game.

In the next 2 chapters you will learn to decipher statistics in the newspaper, and see some of the **RECORDS** held by the most noteworthy professional and college players.

DECIPHERING STATISTICS IN THE NEWSPAPER

Each day during the basketball season, most newspapers print much information about *NBA* and college teams. There are *team standings*, showing how each team is performing in terms of wins and losses, and there are summaries of each game played the previous day called *game summaries* or *box scores*. The labeled examples here will help you learn to read all of these with ease.

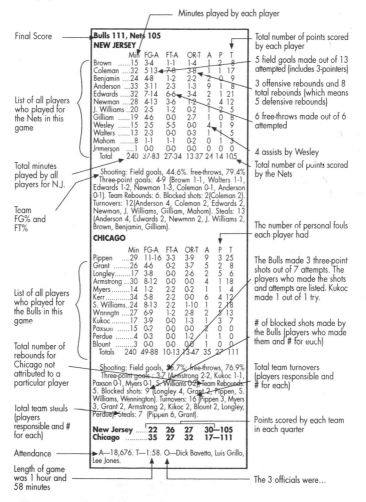

Minutes played by each player

Final Score

Bulls 111, Nets 105
NEW JERSEY

	Min	FG-A	FT-A	OR-T	A	P	T
Brown	15	3-4	1-1	1-4	1	2	8
Coleman	32	5 13	7-8	3-8	1	1	17
Benjamin	24	4-8	1-2	2-2	2	0	9
Anderson	33	3-11	2-3	1-3	9	1	8
Edwards	32	7-14	6-6	3-4	2	1	21
Newman	28	4-13	3-6	1-2	2	4	12
J. Williams	20	2-5	1-2	0-2	1	2	5
Gilliam	19	4-6	0-0	2-7	1	0	8
Wesley	15	2-5	5-5	0-0	4	1	9
Walters	13	2-3	0-0	0-3	1	1	5
Mahom	8	1-1	1-1	0-2	0	1	3
Jnmerson	1	0-0	0-0	0-0	0	0	0
Total	240	37-83	27-34	13-37	24	14	105

Shooting: Field goals, 44.6%. free-throws, 79.4%. Three-point goals: 4-9 (Brown 1-1, Walters 1-1, Edwards 1-2, Newman 1-3, Coleman 0-1, Anderson 0-1). Team Rebounds: 6. Blocked shots: 2(Coleman 2). Turnovers: 12(Anderson 4, Coleman 2, Edwards 2, Newman, J. Williams, Gilliam, Mahom). Steals: 13 (Anderson 4, Edwards 2, Newman 2, J. Williams 2, Brown, Benjamin, Gilliam).

CHICAGO

	Min	FG-A	FT-A	OR-T	A	P	T
Pippen	29	11-16	3-3	3-9	9	3	25
Grant	26	4-6	0-2	3-7	5	2	8
Longley	17	3-8	0-0	2-6	2	5	6
Armstrong	30	8-12	0-0	0-0	4	1	18
Myers	14	1-2	2-2	0-2	1	1	4
Kerr	34	5-8	2-2	0-0	6	4	12
S. Williams	24	8-13	2-2	1-10	1	2	18
Wnnngtn	27	6-9	1-2	2-8	2	5	13
Kukoc	17	3-9	0-0	1-3	1	3	7
Paxson	15	0-2	0-0	0-0	2	0	0
Perdue	4	0-3	0-0	1-2	1	1	0
Blount	3	0-0	0-0	0-0	0	1	0
Totals	240	49-88	10-13	13-47	35	27	111

Shooting: Field goals, 96.7%. free-throws, 76.9%. Three-point goals : 3-7 (Armstrong 2-2, Kukoc 1-1, Paxson 0-1, Myers 0-1, S. Williams 0-2). Team Rebounds: 5. Blocked shots: 9 (Longley 4, Grant 2, Pippen, S. Williams, Wennington). Turnovers: 16 (Pippen 3, Myers 3, Grant 2, Armstrong 2, Kikoc 2, Blount 2, Longley, Perdue). Steals: 7 (Pippen 6, Grant).

New Jersey	22	26	27	30	105
Chicago	35	27	32	17	111

A—18,676. T—1:58. O—Dick Bavetta, Luis Grillo, Lee Jones.

Left-side labels:

List of all players who played for the Nets in this game

Total minutes played by all players for N.J.

Team FG% and FT%

List of all players who played for the Bulls in this game

Total number of rebounds for Chicago not attributed to a particular player

Total team steals (players responsible and # for each)

Attendance

Length of game was 1 hour and 58 minutes

Right-side labels:

Total number of points scored by each player

5 field goals made out of 13 attempted (includes 3-pointers)

3 offensive rebounds and 8 total rebounds (which means 5 defensive rebounds)

6 free-throws made out of 6 attempted

4 assists by Wesley

Total number of points scored by the Nets

The number of personal fouls each player had

The Bulls made 3 three-point shots out of 7 attempts. The players who made the shots and attempts are listed. Kukoc made 1 out of 1 try.

# of blocked shots made by the Bulls (players who made them and # for each)

Total team turnovers (players responsible and # for each)

Points scored by each team in each quarter

The 3 officials were...

Number of games lost to date in the season

Win-Loss Percentage

Number of games a team is behind the division leader

Number of games won to date in the season

Number of games won in a row

STANDINGS

NATIONAL BASKETBALL ASSN.

WESTERN CONFERENCE

Win-Loss record on home court

Win-Loss record while on the road

The order of teams is determined by the win-loss percentage

Pacific Div.	W	L	Pct.	GB	Streak	Home	Away
y-Seattle	58	18	.763	—	Won 3	34-4	24-14
x-Phoenix	50	26	.658	8	Won 1	32-5	18-21
x-Golden State	45	31	.593	13	Won 3	25-12	20-19
x-Portland	45	31	.592	13½	Lost 1	30-9	15-22
Lakers	33	42	.440	24	Lost 3	21-17	12-25
Clippers	26	50	.342	32	Lost 4	16-21	10-29
Sacramento	26	50	.342	32	Lost 1	19-20	7-30

Add W+L to get # of games played so far in the season (52+23=78)

Midwest Div.	W	L	Pct.	GB	Streak	Home	Away
x-Houston	55	20	.733	—	Won 5	33-5	22-15
x-San Antonio	53	23	.697	2½	Won 1	31-7	22-16
x-Utah	48	28	.632	7½	Won 3	31-8	17-20
Denver	37	38	.493	18	Lost 2	27-12	10-26
Minnesota	20	56	.263	35½	Lost 4	13-25	7-33
Dallas	10	66	.132	45½	Won 1	3-33	7-33

EASTERN CONFERENCE

Since 7 teams have clinched a playoff berth (y)(x) only 1 more team in the Western Conference will be in the playoffs while 3 more teams are still vying for playoff berths in the Eastern Division.

Atlantic Div.	W	L	Pct.	GB	Streak	Home	Away
x-New York	52	23	.693	—	Lost 3	30-8	22-15
x-Orlando	46	29	.613	6	Won 4	28-9	18-20
Miami	40	36	.526	12½	Lost 2	20-17	20-19
New Jersey	40	36	.526	12½	Lost 1	27-12	13-24
Boston	28	47	.373	24	Lost 1	15-22	13-25
Philadelphia	24	52	.316	28½	Won 1	14-24	10-28
Washington	22	53	.293	30	Lost 1	15-22	7-31

Central Div.	W	L	Pct.	GB	Streak	Home	Away
x-Atlanta	52	23	.693	—	Won 1	33-5	19-18
x-Chicago	52	24	.684	½	Won 8	30-8	22-16
x-Cleveland	43	33	.566	9½	Won 1	28-10	15-23
Indiana	40	35	.533	12	Won 1	26-12	14-23
Charlotte	36	39	.480	16	Won 4	25-12	11-27
Detroit	20	55	.267	32	Lost 6	10-29	10-26
Milwaukee	19	56	.253	33	Lost 5	10-26	9-30

x-clinched playoff berth; y-clinched division title

Sometimes college scores are reported in this way to conserve space:

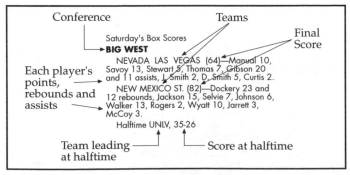

Conference

Teams

Final Score

Saturday's Box Scores
BIG WEST
NEVADA LAS VEGAS (64)—Manual 10, Savoy 13, Stewart 3, Thomas 7, Gibson 20 and 11 assists, J. Smith 2, D. Smith 5, Curtis 2.
NEW MEXICO ST. (82)—Dockery 23 and 12 rebounds, Jackson 15, Selvie 7, Johnson 6, Walker 13, Rogers 2, Wyatt 10, Jarrett 3, McCoy 3.
Halftime UNLV, 35-26

Each player's points, rebounds and assists

Team leading at halftime

Score at halftime

NBA & COLLEGE RECORDS

(*=player is still active; statistics current through end of 1993-94 Season)

PROFESSIONAL SCORING LEADERS

All-Time Career Scoring Leaders (NBA only)

Player	Points	Years
Abdul-Jabbar, Kareem	38,387	1969-89
Chamberlain, Wilt	31,419	1959-73
Malone, Moses*	27,360	1976-94
Hayes, Elvin	27,313	1968-84
Robertson, Oscar	26,710	1960-74
Havlicek, John	26,395	1962-78
English, Alex	25,613	1976-91
West, Jerry	25,192	1960-74
Wilkins, Dominique*	24,019	1982-94
Dantley, Adrian	23,177	1976-91
Baylor, Elgin	23,149	1958-72

All-Time Points Per Game (PPG) Leaders

Player	PPG	Years
Jordan, Michael	32.3	1984-93
Chamberlain, Wilt	30.1	1959-73
Baylor, Elgin	27.4	1958-72
West, Jerry	27.0	1960-74
Wilkins, Dominique*	26.5	1982-94

Most Seasons Leading the League in Scoring

Player	#Seasons	Years
Chamberlain, Wilt	7	1959-66
Jordan, Michael	7	1986-93

Most Points in a Single Season

Player	Points	Years	Player	Points	Season
Chamberlain, Wilt	4,029	1961-62	Jordan, Michael	2,868	1987-88
Chamberlain, Wilt	3,586	1962-63	McAdoo, Bob	2,831	1974-75
Jordan, Michael	3,041	1986-87	Barry, Rick	2,775	1966-67
Chamberlain, Wilt	3,033	1960-61	Jordan, Michael	2,753	1989-90
Chamberlain, Wilt	2,948	1963-64	Baylor, Elgin	2,719	1962-63

Most Points in a Single Game

Player	Points	Date	Player	Points	Date
Chamberlain, Wilt	100	3/2/62	Chamberlain, Wilt	72	11/3/62
Chamberlain, Wilt	78	12/8/61	Baylor, Elgin	71	11/15/60
Chamberlain, Wilt	73	1/13/62	Robinson, David*	71	4/24/94
Chamberlain, Wilt	73	11/16/62	Chamberlain, Wilt	70	3/10/63
Thompson, David	73	4/9/78	Jordan, Michael	69	3/28/90

THREE-POINT SHOOTING

Most Career 3-Point Field Goals (only calculated since 1979-80)

Player	3-PT FGs	Years
Ellis, Dale*	1013	1983-1994

Most 3-Point Field Goals in a Single Season

Player	3-PT FGs	Season
Majerle, Dan*	192	1993-94
Maxwell, Vernon*	172	1990-91

FREE-THROW SHOOTING

Highest Career Free-Throw Percentages (min. 1,200 FTs made)

Player	%	Years
Price, Mark*	.908	1986-94
Barry, Rick	.900	1965-80
Murphy, Calvin	.892	1970-83
Bird, Larry	.886	1979-92

ASSISTS

Most Career Assists

Player	Assists	Years
Johnson, Magic	9,921	1979-92
Robertson, Oscar	9,887	1960-74
Stockton, John*	9,383	1984-94
Thomas, Isiah	9,061	1981-94
Cheeks, Maurice	7,392	1978-91

Most Assists in a Single Season

Player	Assists	Season
Stockton, John*	1,164	1990-91
Stockton, John*	1,134	1989-90
Stockton, John*	1,128	1987-88
Stockton, John*	1,126	1991-92
Thomas, Isiah	1,123	1984-85

REBOUNDS

(compiled since 1951/offensive/defensive distinction only since 1973-74)

Most Career Rebounds (includes ABA)

Player	Rebounds	Years
Chamberlain, Wilt	23,924	1959-73
Russell, Bill	21,620	1956-69
Malone, Moses*	17,788	1976-94
Abdul-Jabbar, Kareem	17,440	1969-89
Gilmore, Artis	16,330	1971-88

Most Rebounds in a Single Game

Player	Rebounds	Date
Chamberlain, Wilt	55	11/24/60
Russell, Bill	51	2/8/60

STEALS (compiled only since 1973-74)

Most Career Steals

Player	Steals	Years
Cheeks, Maurice	2,310	1978-91

Most Steals in a Single Season

Player	Steals	Season
Robertson, Alvin	301	1985-86

BLOCKED SHOTS (compiled only since 1973-74)

Most Career Blocked Shots

Player	Blocks	Years
Abdul-Jabbar, Kareem	3,189	1973-89
Eaton, Mark	3,064	1982-93

Most Blocked Shots in a Single Season

Player	Points	Season
Eaton, Mark	456	1984-85
Bol, Manute	397	1985-86
Smith, Elmore	393	1973-74

Most Blocked Shots in a Single Game

Player	Blocks	Dates
Smith, Elmore	17	10/28/73
Bol, Manute	15	1/25/86 and 2/26/87

COLLEGE SCORING AND ASSIST LEADERS

Most Points in a Single Game

Player	Points	Division	Date
Francis, Clarence "Bevo"	113	Div. II	2/2/54
Selvy, Frank	100	Div. I	2/13/54
Bradshaw, Kevin	72	Div. I	1/5/91

Most Points in a Single Season

Player	Points	Division	Season
Maravich, Pete	1,381	Div. I	1969-70

Most Career Points

Player	Points	Division	Years
Grant, Travis	4,045	Div. II	1969-72
Maravich, Pete	3,667	Div. I	1968-70

Most Career Assists

Player	Points	Division	Years
Hurley, Bobby	1,076	Div. I	1990-93

GREAT TEAMS & DYNASTIES

HALL OF FAME TEAMS

Original Celtics: created in a tough New York City neighborhood in 1914, they were considered the greatest of the early pro teams. They reluctantly joined the *ABL* when it was formed in 1925 only after they faced bankruptcy when other teams refused to play them. Over a 10 year period they traveled through 13 states, winning 1320 games while losing only 66. They are credited with inventing some of the most creative moves still used today (e.g., *pivot* plays, switching defenses).

Harlem Globetrotters: This all-black team, born in 1926, was the vision of Abe Saperstein, their Jewish immigrant coach, who saw great potential in the hard-working players he originally brought together to play serious games. The team turned to entertaining with trick shots, fancy passes and dribbling stunts that audiences seemed to enjoy more. They choose their name to announce they were black (they were really from Chicago) and to make people think they had traveled extensively. The team still exists, amusing fans around the world and acting as goodwill ambassadors for basketball.

The N.Y. Renaissance (*Rens*): Considered the best basketball team in the U.S. between 1932-1936, they amassed an 88-game win streak (1934) and an overall record of 473-49. This all-black team traveled for 4 months a year, usually sleeping on the team bus as hotels refused to accommodate them. Organized in Harlem in 1922, the team lasted 27 years, often playing 2 or 3 games a day.

NBA TEAMS

Boston Celtics: They still hold the record for the most *NBA* titles — 16 — won from 1957 to date (1957, 1959-66, 1968-69, 1974, 1976, 1981, 1984, 1986) and the most consecutive titles — 8 — in their 19 appearances at the NBA *Finals*. Defense and clever passing was their trademark.

Chicago Bulls: The 1st team to win 3 consecutive NBA titles since the 1960s was led to victory by *Michael Jordan* in 1991, 1992 and 1993. His retirement is probably the only thing that stopped the streak, as the team reached the Eastern Conference Finals even in his absence.

Los Angeles Lakers: This *franchise* has been a winner since the first days of the NBA — with 6 trips to the Finals and 5 NBA titles (1949, 1950, 1952-54) while still in Minneapolis, then 6 more titles (1972, 1979, 1981, 1985, 1987 and 1988) in 18 trips to the Finals from L.A. Their 33-game winning streak in 1971-72 is still a record. Under coach *Patrick Riley*, they dominated the 1980s.

COLLEGE TEAMS

CCNY (City College of N.Y.): Although known more as an academic than an athletic college, CCNY's basketball teams were remarkable (a 36-4 record from 1922-25 and a 43-3 record from 1931-34). It is the only team to win both the *NCAA Tournament* and *NIT* in one year (1950) to be crowned undisputed college champion. Unfortunately, most of that team's members were involved in the 1950's *point-shaving* scandal (where players at several colleges accepted bribes to win games by less than the *point spread*) which rocked the college and pro sport for years with allegations of crookedness.

Duke University Blue Devils: In an incredible 9-year stretch, coach *Mike Krzyzewski* has brought them to the *Final Four* 7 times, the final game 5 times and won 2 titles (1991 and 1992). Their 60-week streak ranked as one of the top 10 college teams in the nation started January 21, 1991 and continues to this day. They are still tied with UNLV (37-2 in 1987) for the most wins in a single season (37-3 in 1986).

Indiana University Hoosiers: the entire state of Indiana participates in "Hoosier Hysteria." The team has won 5 NCAA titles (2nd to *UCLA*), 3 under *Bobby Knight* (1976, 1981 and 1987). In his 23 years there, Knight has led them to 11 Big 10 titles, 17 NCAA Tournaments, 5 Final Four appearances and 1 NIT title. His teams have had 16 seasons with 20 or more wins while amassing a .759 *winning percentage.*

UCLA (University of California Los Angeles) Bruins: Under Coach *John Wooden* the Bruins won a record 10 NCAA championships (7 consecutive) from 1964-75 . They had a 3-year, 88-game unbeaten streak (1971-74), an unprecedented 38-straight wins in NCAA Tournament play and went undefeated 4 seasons (1963-64, 1966-67, 1971-73). It was the first team to use a *full-court press* successfully.

HALL OF FAME

First conceived as a shrine to the game's founder *Dr. James Naismith* when he died in 1939, The Naismith Memorial Basketball *Hall of Fame* first opened on February 18, 1968 in Springfield, Massachusetts (although its first elections had been held nearly a decade earlier in 1959!). Its original site on the Springfield College campus proved inadequate so a modernized, three-story complex on the Connecticut River (still in Springfield) became its new home in 1985. Photos, memorabilia and movies honor basketball greats at every level — high school, college, Olympic and professional.

Individuals are nominated on an annual basis in one of 4 categories: player (5 years after retirement), *coach* (after 25 years in the profession), *referee* (5 years after retirement) and contributor (at any time). The Honors Committee, comprised of 24 members representing many facets of basketball, vote; a minimum of 18 votes is required for induction. Five members are selected annually (in November) and inducted in May of the following year.

Only one individual, *John Wooden*, has been selected twice, first as a player (1960) and then as a coach (1972). Bill Bradley was inducted when he was a U.S. Senator in 1982. In addition to the 201 individuals enshrined through 1994, 4 teams have been selected: the First Team to play in 1891, the *Original Celtics*, the Buffalo Germans and the New York Renaissance (*Rens*).

TROPHIES AND AWARDS

NBA

Maurice Podoloff Trophy: awarded during the *post-season* to the league's *Most Valuable Player* (*MVP*) of the season, this trophy was named after the *NBA*'s first *Commissioner*. Selected by a vote of NBA players from 1955-56 through 1979-80; since 1980-81 the player has been selected by the Writers and Broadcasters. Won a record 6 times by *Kareem Abdul-Jabbar*; other notables include *Bill Russell* (5 wins); *Wilt Chamberlain* (4 wins); and 3 times each by: *Moses Malone, Larry Bird, Magic Johnson* and *Michael Jordan.*

Red Auerbach Trophy: Awarded to the *Coach of the Year* as selected by the Writers and Broadcasters since 1962-63. Only 1 coach, Don Nelson, has won it 3 times. Bill Fitch (Cleveland, Boston), Cotton Fitzimmons (Kansas City, Phoenix), Gene Shue (Baltimore, Washington) and *Patrick Riley* (*L. A. Lakers*, New York Knicks) have each won it twice.

Eddie Gottlieb Trophy: the NBA *Rookie of the Year* has been selected by the Writers and Broadcasters after the season ends since 1952-53. Not every player awarded this honor has gone on to a great pro career. The best include *Elgin Baylor*, Wilt Chamberlain, *Oscar Robertson*, Kareem Abdul-Jabbar, Larry Bird, *Patrick Ewing*, *Rick Barry* and Michael Jordan. Likewise, some of the most illustrious NBA careers did not start with this honor, such as Magic Johnson's.

Defensive Player of the Year: In 1982-83, the Writers and Broadcasters decided it was time to honor the player who exhibited the best defensive skills throughout the season. To date, Sidney Montcrief and Dennis Rodman are the only players to win it twice. Although Michael Jordan is better known for his scoring ability his receiving this award is testimony to his versatility.

Sixth Man Award: Since 1982-83, the Writers and Broadcasters have recognized the greatest *sixth man* of the NBA. Kevin McHale, Ricky Pierce and Detlef Schrempf were each honored twice.

Most Improved Player: In 1985-86, the Writers and Broadcasters began honoring the player who most improved from the beginning of each season to its final game.

Larry O'Brien Trophy: named in honor of the *NBA*'s third Commissioner, it is awarded to the team that wins the NBA *Finals*; presented by the Commissioner at the end of the *series*.

NBA Finals MVP: Since 1969, given to the player credited with being the most valuable based on his contribution in the Finals series, as selected by a media panel. Though generally bestowed on a member of the winning team, *Jerry West* of the *L.A. Lakers* won it in 1969 even though the *Boston Celtics* were crowned champions.

Executive of the Year: selected by the Sporting News to recognize the best owner or management person in the NBA.

J. Walter Kennedy Citizenship Award: Since 1974-75, the Pro Basketball Writers Association of America has recognized one individual involved with basketball each year for his contributions to the outside community.

IBM Award (formerly the *Schick Award*): A computer formula which considers key offensive and defensive characteristics determines the player most valuable to his team. Since its inception in 1983-84, either Magic Johnson, Michael Jordan, *Charles Barkley* or *David Robinson* has won it.

All-Rookie Team: Selected by the NBA coaches since 1962-63, this imaginary team combines the best 2 *forwards*, 2 *guards* and *center* of the rookie class. Since 1988-89, there is now a First Team and Second Team honoring the 10 best rookies each year.

All-Defensive Team: Since 1968-69, the NBA coaches select a First Team and Second Team (each with a center, 2 guards and 2 forwards) from all active NBA players to create the best imaginary defensive unit.

All-NBA Team: Both the First Team and Second Team have been selected by the Writers and Broadcasters since 1946-47. Beginning in 1988-89, a Third Team was added. Each of these 3 imaginary teams aims to combine the best 2 guards, 2 forwards and center in the NBA based on overall performance.

COLLEGE

All-America Team: Selected by the Associated Press at the end of each *regular season*, the imaginary First, Second and Third Teams each have 5 of the top players (each with a center, 2 guards and 2 forwards).

There are actually 4 separate *Player of the Year* awards presented to college athletes at the end of the *regular season* in March:

Adolph F. Rupp Trophy: since 1972, this solid bronze trophy is presented annually to the player selected by the Associated Press; it was won 3 years in a row by Ralph Samson (University of Virginia 1981-83).

John Wooden Award: presented by the L.A. Athletic Club, it honors one of 16 finalists as the top player of the year, as voted by over 1,000 sportswriters and broadcasters.

Naismith Player of the Year: awarded to one of 5 finalists this award was conceived by the Atlanta Tipoff Club in 1969. First won by Kareem Abdul-Jabbar, its only 3-time winners are *Bill Walton* (1972-74) and Ralph Sampson (1981-83).

Eastman Award: awarded to the player of the year as selected by the National Association of Basketball Coaches.

PERSONALITIES: PAST & PRESENT

It has been said that *Dr. J* saved the NBA, *Magic Johnson* and *Larry Bird* built the league, and *Michael Jordan* polished it. The biographies in this chapter are meant to provide you with an overview of these and many more of basketball's personalities. Some of its past superstars, potential future stars, coaches, analysts, commentators and even referees, at both the college and professional level, were chosen. So many personalities have graced the game over the last century that limited space prevents us from mentioning them all. Please do not be disappointed if your favorites are not listed here. The statistics in this section are current through the end of the 1993-94 season and this key will help you understand the abbreviations in the entries below:

> A=Active, *FG%=field goal percentage*, HF=*Hall of Fame*, H.S.=High School, *MVP*=Most Valuable Player, *ppg= points-per-game average*, R=Retired

SHORTEST & TALLEST PLAYERS: Muggsy Bogues 5'3" (Charlotte Hornets) and Spud Webb 5'7" (Sacramento Kings) are both active *point guards. Manute Bol* 7'7" was cut by the Philadelphia 76ers in 1993 and replaced by Shawn Bradley 7'6".

OLDEST PLAYERS: *Robert "the Chief" Parish* just signed a multi-year contract with the Charlotte Hornets at age 41, so he is likely to be older at retirement than *Kareem Abdul-Jabbar* was (age 42 at his 1989 retirement). Parish was a 9-time *All-Star center* in his long career with the *Boston Celtics* with whom he won 3 NBA championships.

ABDUL-JABBAR, KAREEM (Center, R): Born in N.Y. as Lewis Alcindor, he grew up to be "the most dominant player in his lifetime," according to *John Wooden* who coached the 3-time *All-American* at *UCLA* to 3 consecutive *NCAA* titles (1967-69) where Lew was named *Final Four* MVP in each. When the NCAA instituted a no-*dunk* rule to stop him, it only made him more creative offensively and a devastating defender. At 7'2" he developed the unstoppable *skyhook*. This unselfish player had an incredible 20-year NBA career with the Milwaukee Bucks and *L.A. Lakers* — the longest to date — retiring in 1989 at the age of 42. The 1st overall pick in the *draft*, he was *Rookie of the Year* (1969-70), *NBA Finals* MVP twice and league MVP a record 6 times, while setting career records for seasons, games and minutes played, field goals attempted and made, shots blocked and points. He won 6 championship rings, 4 in his last 8 seasons.

In 1968, he refused to participate in the Olympics on political grounds. Always a very private person, he put off the media until his later years. Today, the 47-year old is president of Kareem Productions, an L.A. entertainment company that produces movies about the black experience. He is also keeping busy as a father, businessman, ESPN commentator and actor (Stephen King wrote in a role for him in "The Stand", and he has had bit parts in "Fletch", "Airplane" and "The Mighty Ducks") and with anti-gang/stay-in-school projects.

AUERBACH, RED (Coach, R, HF): The NBA's most hated and respected coach is best known for the cigar he lit after each *Boston Celtics* victory, a ritual symbolic of his defiant personality. Under his tutelage the Celtics won a record 13 championships (8 consecutive and 9 out of 10 from 1963-72), as he accumulated a 1037-548 record. Named *Coach of the Year* in 1965, incredibly he never had a losing season in his 20-year career. This success and the advent of televised games brought his behavior into the limelight — the constant stamping of his feet, shouting at *officials* and *technical fouls* led to frequent ejections and fines. He helped break the color barrier in basketball when he selected Chuck Cooper (the first black player to join the NBA) in the 1950 *draft* and again when he appointed *Bill Russell* his successor (the NBA's first black coach) in 1966. Since then, he has been the Celtics' general manager, exhibiting a knack for drafting talent that allows the team to continue winning despite not having a single draft pick higher than #4 in the last 25 years (except the late Len Bias in 1986).

BARKLEY, CHARLES (Forward, A): (**Photo** on p. 33) A H.S. coach called this shy, quiet teenager "average." At Auburn University he was criticized for being lazy. Yet, the "Round Mound of *Rebound*", an overweight 5th *draft* pick in 1984, became known as "Sir Charles", a outspoken, aggressive NBA superstar whose favorite subject is himself. He is the Philadelphia 76ers' all-time leading rebounder (he thinks "any knucklehead can score ... rebounding is special, it's desire"). The year his tumultuous relationship with the 76ers ended in a trade, a liberated Barkley averaged 24.1 *ppg* for the Phoenix Suns, nearly upset the defending champion *Chicago Bulls* in the *playoffs* and was named league MVP (1992-93). This 8-time *All-Star* was also a member of the 1992 Olympic *Dream Team* and is a 3-time *Schick Award* recipient. At times he has also been "Sir Jerk", spitting on a fan in 1992 and making headlines with two bar scuffles. Despite chronic back problems and frequent hints of retirement, he will return for at least 1 more season in his quest for the elusive championship ring which to him is "the only thing that matters." After that, he will pursue politics or acting. His outrageous personality is sure to provide entertainment, whatever he chooses.

BARRY, RICK (Forward, R, HF): This sharpshooter from the University of Miami led the *NCAA* in scoring but was thought too skinny for the NBA's physical play. The San Francisco Warriors' 1964 *draft* pick promptly proved his critics wrong — he amassed 850 *rebounds* and 25.7 *ppg* (4th in the league) that season, was named *Rookie of the Year* and dethroned *Wilt Chamberlain* as scoring champion in Barry's 2nd year. A controversial, cocky player with a quick temper, he mellowed with time. In 1967 he was the only superstar to defect to the newly-formed *ABA*, to play for his college coach/father-in-law. A court order forced him to sit out 1 year, but he returned to lead that team, and later the N.J. Nets, to ABA championships. He was a 4-time All-ABA Team selection (1968-72) before a court ordered him to rejoin the NBA. Best remembered for his underhanded *free-throw shooting*, he is still 2nd in career *free-throw percentage* (.900). He is currently a candid, critical basketball analyst.

BAYLOR, ELGIN (Forward, R, HF): His successful mix of agility and muscle made him a great scorer and powerful *rebounder* known for his relentless pursuit of the ball. A twitch of the head easily identified this *All-American* out of Seattle University who was picked 1st overall in the 1958-59 draft by the Minneapolis Lakers. In his first year he was 4th in league scoring and 3rd in rebounding, and was named *Rookie of the Year* and co-MVP of the *All-Star Game*. He spent his entire 14-year career with the *Lakers*, moving to L.A. in 1960-61 where he combined efforts with *Jerry West* in what was then considered the best tandem in NBA history. Two years before *Wilt Chamberlain*, it was Baylor who set and broke the record for most points in a single game (63, then 64, then 71). Trouble with calcium deposits in his knees began in 1964 but his illustrious career continued through 1971, when he retired as the Lakers' all-time leading scorer (23,149 points). Baylor was an assistant, then head coach for the New Orleans Jazz until he was fired in 1979. The L.A. Clippers took him on as a special assistant in 1984 and in 1986 he became general manager. Today, he is still leading the *franchise* through its series of coaching changes and malcontent players.

BIRD, LARRY (Forward, R): (**Photo** on p. 28): One of the players responsible for revitalizing the NBA, he actually agonized over his career decision — whether to play ball or be a gas station attendant. He chose the NBA, mastering the no-look *pass*, game-winning shot and in-traffic *rebound*. As a H.S. senior in French Lick, Indiana, he was recruited by a Florida college but was too terrified to get on a plane, so he stayed home. In fact, he was too awed to attend Indiana State University until after a few months at a community college. Always an intensely private person, he became wary of the media when he was misquoted early in his difficult personal life (his father committed suicide, a brief marriage ended in divorce and his ex-wife filed a paternity suit, all before 1976).

The *Boston Celtics* were so convinced of his talent they used a 1st *round draft* pick to select him in his junior year, though he refused to leave college early. During his career he was *Rookie of the Year* (1979-80), 3-time league MVP, selected 9 times as an *All-Star Game* starter, 11 times to the *All-NBA First Team*, twice NBA *Finals* MVP, once All-Star MVP, and was a *Dream Team* gold medalist at the 1992 Olympics. He led what is considered the greatest front line in NBA history (with *Robert Parish* and Kevin McHale), earning 3 NBA titles while appearing in 5 NBA *Finals* during the 1980s. He finished his illustrious career 11th all-time in scoring, 8th in *steals*, 4th in *free-throw percentage*, 4th in 3-pointers made (649) and 2nd only to *Magic Johnson* in career *triple doubles* (59). When a bad back forced him to retire in 1991-92 after 13 seasons, he became a Celtics' special assistant with the role of developing young players.

BOL, MANUTE (Center) (**Photo** on p. 36): This 7'7" Dinka tribesman from Sudan can *dunk* the ball without leaving the floor. He is so thin Woody Allen once joked he could be faxed from city to city to save travel costs. The first foreigner to enter the NBA had not even heard of basketball before 1979. After the playing at the University of Bridgeport and a stint in the *CBA*, he was only the 31st player drafted (the 10th center) in 1985. Yet he led the NBA in *blocked* shots in 1985-86 (4.96 per game — 2nd highest <u>ever</u> in the NBA) and again in 1988-89. In 1990, the Philadelphia 76ers offered him $4.2 million over 4 years. He has developed a terrific sense of humor in English and is involved in political causes to help Africa.

CHAMBERLAIN, WILT (Center, R, HF): "Wilt the Stilt" was a 7'1" powerhouse who broke every scoring record in the NBA, but he was also a moody, introspective player who often missed practice and created tensions with coaches and teammates. In anticipation of his NBA arrival, NBC expanded its game coverage to both Saturday and Sunday. Wilt joined the Philadelphia (later San Francisco) Warriors in 1959 (after a year with the *Harlem Globetrotters* when he left the University of Kansas as a junior) averaging 37.6 *ppg* in his *rookie* season. After being named *Rookie of the Year*, Wilt announced his retirement claiming he had nothing left to prove, and that he preferred to be a successful businessman appreciated for his brains. It was this type of independent and arrogant behavior that caused critics to call him selfish, instead of admiring his accomplishments. Still, his Philadelphia 76ers (traded in 1964) was the only team able to break the *Boston Celtic's* championship winning streak when it took the title in 1967. When he joined the *L.A. Lakers* in 1968, he led them to 33 consecutive victories (still an NBA record) and 2 NBA titles.

Wilt won the scoring title 7 years in a row and led the NBA in rebounding 5 times. He averaged over 50 ppg one season (1961-62) and scored an incredible 100 points in one game! Had he not been such a poor *free-throw shooter* (he holds some of the worst records) he would have been even more devastating. A perennial *All-Team* and *All-Star Game* selection, he was voted league MVP 4 times and NBA *Finals* MVP once. In his recent autobiography he shocked the public when he bragged about sleeping with over 20,000 women.

COLEMAN, DERRICK (Forward A): From Syracuse University, this 1st player selected in the 1990 *draft* is considered one of the best *power forwards* in the NBA by some, highly overrated by others. Surprisingly, he turned down a $67 million contract before agreeing to terms with the N.J. Nets, and tried to become a *free agent* after being named 1991 *Rookie of the Year*. When he re-signed a 5-year $37.5 million deal with the Nets in February 1994, he became the highest-paid NBA player. He made his *All-Star* debut as a starter in 1994, but his trash-talking antics at the 1994 *World Cup* may cost him consideration for the 1996 Olympics.

COUSY, BOB (Guard, R, HF): "Cooz", an *All-American* from Holy Cross College, was one of the most gifted ball handlers in NBA history, dribbling well with either hand or behind his back, and even more adept at passing to set up plays for teammates. This "Houdini of the Hardwood" led the NBA in assists for 8 years (1953-60) and was voted league MVP in 1957. Though a popular college star, *Red Auerbach* thought he was too small and too flashy for the *Boston Celtics*. It was only through the luck of the draw that he landed in Boston, when a 1950 mini-expansion *draft* was held after Cousy's NBA team folded. He toned down his passing style and in time Red beamed "There's <u>nobody</u> as good as Cousy — and there never was." Still, Cooz did not win a championship until *Bill Russell* joined the team, and together they amassed 6 titles. In his 13-year career Cooz was selected to the *All-NBA Team* 10 years in a row and participated in 13 *All-Star Games*. When he retired in 1963 he coached at Boston College and is currently head of the Hall of Fame Screening Committee.

ERVING, JULIUS (Forward, R, HF): Called *"Doctor J"* because of how he "operated" on the court, he went from the University of Massachusetts to the *ABA* for 5 years, then joined the Philadelphia 76ers for 11 seasons in 1976. Dr. J was the first player to make high-flying, acrobatic moves — the *slam dunk* was the trademark of his spectacular, creative play — which were later copied by players like *Michael Jordan*. He was voted ABA MVP 3 years in a row (1974-76), led the ABA in scoring 3 times and was NBA MVP in 1980-81. He scored over 1,000-points in each of his 16 seasons and is 1 of 3 players to score over 30,000 career points. When he retired in 1987, Erving needed to distance himself from the sport that had consumed him since age 8. He became a successful businessman with a Coca-Cola bottling company and a cable TV firm. In 1993, fulfilling the urge to return to the game, he replaced Quinn Buckner as the analyst for NBC's "NBA Showtime." He will be remembered as the player who stepped forward when the NBA was losing credibility, participating in countless charities and bringing a positive attitude to all he did. Named Sportsman of the Decade, he is still one of the sport's greatest ambassadors.

EWING, PATRICK (Center, A): This powerful and enigmatic Jamaican immigrant has evolved considerably offensively since he led Georgetown to the 1984 *NCAA* title as *Final Four* MVP. He was *Rookie of the Year* (1985-86), a 4-time *All-Star* starter and also a gold medalist with the 1992 Olympic *Dream Team*. Fickle N.Y. fans first clamored for the Knicks to trade him, then lauded him as the best center in the NBA. In truth, he consistently ranks just behind *Hakeem Olajuwon* statistically, with career averages of 23.8 *ppg*, 10.3 *rebounds*, 2.9 *blocks* and 52.2 *FG%*. Ten years into his career, product endorsements continued to elude him, so he started his own sneaker manufacturing company, Ewing Athletics Co. He is integrally involved in the marketing efforts of the company, which boasts $60 million in worldwide sales and is growing rapidly. This devoted family man, contrary to his public image, is charming, funny and gentle, and his generosity to charities is rarely noted by the press.

HURLEY, BOBBY (Guard, A): The NBA's most closely-watched comeback story, he nearly died when he was thrown from his car in an accident on the way home from a game in December 1993. He played in 140 games for *Duke University* (1990-93), breaking the NCAA career *assists* record (1,076), bringing the Blue Devils to the finals 3 times to win 2 championships and winning a *Final Four* MVP award (1992). This 7th pick of the 1993 *draft* signed a 6-year $16.2 million contract with the Sacramento Kings for whom he played just 7 weeks before his accident. He is now a spokesman for wearing seat belts and with his tireless drive is expected to make a complete recovery.

JOHNSON, EARVIN (Guard, R): He was simply *Magic* (or Buck or Junior to his friends). Always beaming his famous smile, he introduced teamwork to pro-basketball, making the no-look pass his signature. At 6'9" he revolutionized the *point guard* position previously reserved for smaller players with his unsurpassed *court vision*. Magic's record-setting 137 *triple doubles* are a testimony to both his unselfishness and ever-expanding skills. Whether it was scoring, *rebounding*, ball handling or leadership, Magic excelled as no other player had. His decade-long rivalry with *Larry Bird* began in college (when as a sophomore Magic led Michigan State to the *NCAA* title over Bird's team) and aided the NBA's rebirth. As a million dollar *rookie* in 1979, Magic led the *L.A. Lakers* to the championship, scoring 42 points while playing <u>every</u> position in the final game. During his 12-year career, he led the team to 9 NBA *Finals* and 5 titles, was named *Finals* MVP and league MVP 3 times each, and left the NBA ranked 1st in assists (9,921) and 2nd in steals (1,698).

He retired at the start of the 1991-92 season with the announcement that he was HIV-positive, and became a spokesman for the disease as a member of the National Commission on AIDS and through his free video on safe sex. His brief comeback attempt was fraught with controversy as players grappled with the thought of infectious diseases on the court. Though retired, fans voted him to an appearance in the 1992 *All-Star Game* where he was named MVP, and that summer he won an Olympic gold medal with the *Dream Team*. He coached the Lakers for the last 16 games of the 1993-94 season, then became a team vice-president when he purchased a 5% interest in the Lakers for $10-$15 million, realizing part of his dream to own an NBA *franchise*. He is a savvy businessman with investment positions in many of the companies whose products he endorsed. With his philosophy that "Sometimes you just need to look for the positive side of things" he has become an international hero and a role model for young black men. Magic is currently a color analyst for NBC.

JOHNSON, LARRY (Forward, A): This member of the 1990 *NCAA* champion UNLV Runnin' Rebels made an immediate impact in the NBA, helping turn around the Charlotte Hornets. He was named *Rookie of the Year* (1991-92) for his steady scoring and *rebounding*, started as an *All-Star* (1992-93) and was a member of *Dream Team II* in 1994. To assure he did not become a *free agent* in 1998, the Hornets re-signed him to a 12-year, $84 million deal that made him the highest paid player ever. A back operation in just his 2nd season may shorten a promising career.

JORDAN, MICHAEL (Guard, R): "Air Jordan" defied gravity as he soared toward the basket with his tongue hanging out of his mouth. For 9 years, fans gazed in awe at the perfect basketball player, the most complete package of grace, creativity and athleticism. Though he was *Rookie of the Year* (1984-85), *Defensive Player of the Year* (1987-88) and league MVP (1987-88 for the 1st of 3 times), it took him 7 seasons to win an NBA title. He then led the *Chicago Bulls* to 3 in a row, winning *Finals* MVP honors each time. He led the NBA in scoring 7 consecutive years starting in 1986-87 (he has the highest career *ppg* average with 32.3) and in *steals* 3 times. Jordan also has 2 Olympic gold medals, one from the 1992 *Dream Team*.

Jordan's surprise retirement in October 1993 (who felt he had "reached the pinnacle of [his] career") came after growing rumors about his gambling problems and the bizarre carjacking murder of his father. He will be most remembered for his heart, his relentless drive, and his ability to single-handedly guarantee a win in the closing minutes of a game. His charm enabled him to become a marketing machine — in 1992-93, in addition to a $3.9 million salary he reportedly earned $32 million in endorsements — and he ranks as the #1-most esteemed athlete to kids 12 to 17. He is currently playing baseball for the minor league Birmingham Barons trying to live out his dream of playing major league baseball. Though his baseball career is off to a rocky start — he is batting only .195, and hit only 2 home runs in more than 300 at-bats — Jordan was a slow starter in basketball too as he was cut from his freshman H.S. team, so only time will tell.

KIDD, JASON (Guard, A): This *All-American* left UC Berkeley after just 2 years and was *drafted* 2nd overall by the Dallas Mavericks (9-year $60-million) who hope he can turn around the NBA's worst team. Considered the finest *point guard* prospect since *Magic Johnson* in 1979 he has good court vision and shot selection — he is expected to rival *John Stockton* as the best passer in the NBA. In his last college season, he averaged 16.7 points, 9.1 *assists*, 6.9 *rebounds* and 3.1 *steals* per game after leading the *NCAA* in steals his freshman year.

KNIGHT, BOB (Coach, A): This mercurial college coach has spent the last 28 years coaching, 22 seasons with the *Indiana Hoosiers* after spending 6 years with Army. His winning percentage is 4th best among active *NCAA* coaches (619-214 for a .743 percentage). A perennial NCAA tournament participant, he has brought his Indiana team to 5 *Final Four* appearances and won 3 titles. He has a notoriously bad temper, once throwing a chair onto the court to protest an *official*'s call. His controversial run-ins with players and the media extended to his family last season when he struck his son (who plays for the Hoosiers) for making an error during a game.

KRZYZEWSKI, MIKE (Coach, A): (Pronounced Shuh-chef-ski) Simply called "Coach K" by most, this extremely popular and respected disciple of *Bob Knight* has imprinted his own successful style at *Duke University*, leading the Blue Devils to 7 *Final Four* appearances, 3 final games and 2 NCAA titles (1991 and 1992) in just 9 years. Though lured by the NBA in 1994, he felt more comfortable at Duke where he takes a personal interest in assuring his "kids" graduate. He signed a 15-year $6.6 million endorsement contract with Nike at the close of the 1993 season.

MALONE, MOSES (Center, A): This son of a Virginia meat packer never attended college, taught himself the game and became a star through relentless *rebounding* at both ends, winning 6 rebounding titles in 7 years and 3 NBA MVP awards. In the record books he is currently 4th in scoring (29,531), 3rd in rebounding (17,788) and 3rd in career games (1,312). A 12-time NBA *All-Star,* Old Man Malone (age 39) just signed on for his 20th season with the San Antonio Spurs. He considers leading the Philadelphia 76ers to the 1983 NBA title while being named MVP of the *Finals* his greatest personal triumph, when he became the big man needed to complement *Julius Erving.* His first 2 seasons were in the *ABA* and he is the only ABA player active today. He talks little (some mistake his swift rumbling voice for inarticulateness) and compares himself to Columbo.

MARAVICH, PETE (Guard, R, HF): Known for his flashy passes, "Pistol Pete" rewrote the *NCAA* record books while at Louisiana State University. This 3-time *All-American* (1967-70) led in scoring for 3 straight years and still holds the records for single-season scoring (1,381 in 1970) and career points (3,667 in 83 games), averaging an amazing 44.2 *ppg*. He joined the NBA after his junior year, averaging 24.2 points over his career and playing in 5 *All-Star Games*. His offbeat trademark in the NBA was his inability to keep his socks up. He once said, "I don't want to play 10 years in the NBA and die of a heart attack at age 40." Ironically, that is exactly what he did, collapsing during a pick-up game in 1988.

MIKAN, GEORGE (Center, R, HF): The 1st great *center*, Mikan was told by his H.S. coach he was too tall and big, and therefore too clumsy for the game. This 3-time *All-American* at DePaul University went on to dominate the record books, scoring 44 or more points in 9 games and 61 points in a 1952 game. Crowds packed arenas as "Mr. Basketball" led the NBA in scoring 3 years in a row, won 5 NBA titles in 6 years with the Minneapolis Lakers and was voted Top Player of the 1st Half-Century by the Associated Press. As opposing teams searched for a big man to stop him, he forced the NBA to change many of its rules (eliminating *jump balls* after *field goals*, introducing the *24-second clock*, limiting *team fouls* and widening the *foul lane*). He retired in 1956, becoming the *ABA*'s 1st Commissioner in 1967. Recently, he purchased the Chicago Cheetahs of the new roller hockey league, and at age 70 keeps busy with day-to-day duties from personally washing the mascot's suit to increasing attendance.

OLAJUWON, HAKEEM (Center, A): "Hakeem the Dream" started by playing soccer in his native Nigeria, but it was his basketball skills that shined in a spectacular 1993-94 season. He was named NBA MVP and *Defensive Player of the Year* (for the 2nd consecutive season) as he led the Houston Rockets to their 1st NBA title as *Finals* MVP. He led the league in *blocked shots* 3 seasons, is one of only 4 players to achieve a *quadruple double* in NBA history, and boasts career statistics of 23.7 *ppg*, 12.5 *rebounds*, 3.6 blocks and 51.6% *FG%*. In his 2 years at the University of Houston he was named *Final Four* MVP once even though they lost in the final game both years. Since being selected 1st overall in the 1984 *draft*, in 10 years with the Rockets he has been blamed for team losses, accused of faking an injury to get a new contract and forced to stay due to a *salary cap* technicality. He credits being a devout Muslim (the recently added H gives his name an Arabic pronunciation) for the patience to await a new owner and a 4-year $26 million contract extension. The parents of this 9-time *All-Star* consider the sport so violent they have never seen him play in person — they watched him win the NBA title on TV. In 1994, he was named an international spokesman for the NBA.

O'NEAL, SHAQUILLE (Center, A): "Shaq" left Louisiana State University to join the NBA after leading the *NCAA* with 14.7 *rebounds* a game his sophomore year (1990-91) and 5.23 *blocked shots* per game his junior year (2nd best all-time). He was the 1st overall *draft* pick (Orlando Magic), becoming only the 14th *rookie* to start in an *All-Star Game* on his way to *Rookie of the Year* honors (1992-93). His numbers exploded in his 2nd NBA season when he finished 2nd in scoring (28.9 *ppg*), *rebounds* (13.1 per game) and *FG%* (60%). Yet, his constant need to tell the world how great he is led to only lukewarm MVP support. Still, his boyish charm landed booming endorsements ($11.9 million worth added to a $3.3 million salary). With a book, an album and a movie to his name, he is quickly outpacing *Michael Jordan* as the NBA's marketing king.

RILEY, PATRICK (Coach, A): This 47-year old coach of the N.Y. Knicks first made his mark coaching the *L.A. Lakers* (where he also played *guard* in the '70s). "Riles" personifies "Showtime" with his slicked back hair and Armani suits, though he is actually down to earth with a disciplined work ethic. He is a motivational leader, using Shakespearean and Sun-Tzu quotes to inspire his players with great success — incredibly, in 12 NBA seasons he has always finished 1st in his *division* and has the highest *winning percentage* (701-272 for .721). His versatility is evidenced by 2 *Coach of the Year* awards, one with the graceful Lakers (1990), the other in his 1st season with the aggressive Knicks (1993). With the Lakers he went to the NBA *Finals* 7 times in 9 seasons and won 4 titles, and he brought the Knicks there in only his 2nd year. For the 2 years in between, he was Bob Costas' color analyst on NBC. Riley copyrighted the phrase "3-peat" when the Lakers were on a quest of their 3rd consecutive title, but it is Chicago Bull fans that are paying him royalties. Riles, who is a best-selling author and highly-paid speaker, is rumored to keep his watch on West Coast time.

ROBERTSON, OSCAR (Guard, R, HF): No one knew what to expect when the versatile "Big O" had the ball. A strong jumper with incredible body control, a soft, reliable *shooting touch* and an instinct for *steals*, he could pass, *dribble* and *rebound* as well as he could score. He learned the game in basketball-crazed Indiana where he was elected to the National Honor Society, graduating in the top 10% of his H.S. Despite many options, he chose the University of Cincinnati because of its work-training program, but as its 1st black basketball player he suffered many insults. He persevered and in each of his 3 varsity seasons was named *Player of the Year*, breaking 14 NCAA records (including being the 1st to lead in scoring 3 years in a row). He was named *Rookie of the Year* (1960-61) with the Cincinnati Royals as he averaged 30.5 *ppg* (he is still among all-time career scoring leaders), 9.7 *assists* (to lead the NBA, which he did 5 more times) and 10 *rebounds*. Yet, it was not until he joined the Milwaukee Bucks and *Kareem Abdul-Jabbar* that he won an NBA title (1970-71). He was an *All-Star* each of his 14 years and was named All-Star MVP 3 times.

ROBINSON, DAVID (Center, A): Named the "Admiral" because he delayed his NBA career to serve in the Navy, he still holds the *NCAA* record for the most *blocked shots* in a season (207 in 1986), the most in a single game (14) and the highest average in NCAA history (5.91). On offense, he was among the top 20 career scorers (2,669) and once scored 50 points in a game without scoring a *3-point shot*. In the NBA, he was named *Rookie of the Year* (1989-90), *Defensive Player of the Year* (1991-92), won the *Schick Award* twice (1990-91) and led the league in blocked shots average in 1991-92 (4.49). He is one of only 4 players to achieve a *quadruple double* with 34 points, 10 *rebounds*, 10 *assists* and 10 blocks. When Dennis Rodman joined his San Antonio Spurs in 1993, Robinson had his best year yet with 29.1 *ppg* (to lead the NBA), 13 rebounds and 3.3 blocked shots. This true gentleman is a talented pianist and is likely to represent the U.S. team at the 1996 Olympics.

ROBINSON, GLENN (Forward, A): After his junior year at Purdue University, "Big Dog" was *drafted* 1st overall by the Milwaukee Bucks and will likely be the first NBA player offered a $100 million contract. Before the 1994-95 season even starts he will earn over $4 million in endorsements. In 1993-94, he led the *NCAA* in scoring (30.3 average) and *rebounds* (10.2) helping Purdue to a 29-5 season and the Southeast *Regional Semifinals*. He won all 4 of college basketball's *Player of the Year* awards. A consistent *3-point shooter*, equally adept at *posting up* or playing on the *perimeter*, he has been compared to *Larry Bird* after whom he admits he patterns his game. He is polite and professional in interviews — a quiet guy with a good work ethic.

RUPP, ADOLOPH (Coach, R, HF): As the controversial and outspoken coach of the Kentucky University Wildcats, the "Baron's" 875 wins over a 41-year career (1931-1972) make him the winningest coach in *NCAA* history (only *Jerry Tarkanian* has a better *winning percentage*) and his 4 *NCAA* titles (1948, 1949, 1951 and 1958) rank 2nd only to *John Wooden*'s 10. While many feared his iron fist, he was named *Coach of the Year* 4 times and coached the 1948 U.S. Olympic team. Rupp trained players by concentrating on team rather than individual play, producing 7 Olympic gold medalists, 25 *All-Americans* and 26 professional players (more than any other coach). The brown suit he wore to games became his trademark. Though many of his players were involved in the *point-shaving* scandals of the 1950s, Rupp himself was never implicated.

RUSSELL, BILL (Center, R, HF): Russell was not a prolific scorer, (only 15 *ppg* career), but his defensive abilities set him apart. Using a unique combination of height, reflexes and intelligence he became a great *rebounder* and *shot blocker*. He led the University of San Francisco to 55 consecutive victories and 2 *NCAA* titles, then led the *Boston Celtics* to 11 titles in 13 years, was named Player of the Year 5 times (3 in a row 1961-63) and led the NBA in rebounding 4 times. His great rivalry with *Wilt Chamberlain* touched everything (when Wilt got a $100,000 3-year contract, he asked for $100,001). In 1966, Russell become the 1st black coach of a professional team in any major sport when *Red Auerbach* retired, leading the Celtics to 2 more titles (1967-68, 1968-69) before retiring from the game. Although always an outspoken advocate of African-American rights, he strived to be judged as an individual in his historic coaching role. He once appeared in the TV show "Miami Vice."

STERN, DAVID (Commissioner, A): The man responsible for the international marketing of the NBA started as its attorney with a private firm before becoming its 1st legal counsel. In 1983, he borrowed the idea of promising players a percentage of the owner's take from the NFL, expanding the notion to push through the *salary cap* which helped stabilize the floundering league. He astutely encouraged the marketing of league superstars, developed NBA Properties, NBA Entertainment and NBA International divisions, and over the next decade successfully instituted policies and rule changes aimed at broadening the game's appeal. The recent expiration of the league's *collective bargaining agreement* is his greatest challenge. His lauded negotiating and leadership skill will be needed to convince players to keep the salary cap in an era of prosperity.

STOCKTON, JOHN (Guard, A): This 6'1" member of the Utah Jazz (out of Gonzaga University) is considered the best *point guard* in the NBA. He led the league in *assists* 7 years in a row (1987-94 with a 12.6 average in 1993-94) and in *steals* twice (3.21 in 1988-89 and 2.98 in 1991-92). In 1993-94 he surpassed 1,000 assists for a record 6th season (1,031). His terrific passes leave observers scratching their heads in wonderment, and a recent Sports Illustrated poll of NBA coaches listed him as the best passer in the NBA. His consistent lack of *turnovers* further frustrates opponents.

STROM, EARL (Referee, R): One of the most respected *referees* in the NBA, he retired in 1990 after a 29-year career that spanned 5 of the NBA's 6 decades. Although best known for his hard work and fairness (visiting teams won 42.9% of the time when he officiated compared to 30% when other officials handled the game), he was asked by the league to tone down his showmanship. A tempestuous man who saw himself as the last of a dying breed, he once suffered a broken thumb from punching a heckling fan. He died in 1994 at the age of 66 from a brain tumor.

TARKANIAN, JERRY (Coach) *NCAA* sanctions eventually led to his retirement from UNLV in 1992 and he is still embroiled in a series of law suits. But during his 24-year career there (1974-1992) and earlier at Long Beach State (1969-1973), the "Shark" won an NCAA title and amassed an impressive win-loss record (625-122) that gives him the highest all-time *winning percentage* in NCAA history (.837). Despite such success at the college level, he was fired from the NBA after only 20 games with the San Antonio Spurs in 1992-93.

VITALE, DICK (Commentator, A): The most outrageous hoops color man ever "Dicky V" is a bubbly marathon talker who rarely inhales. His unmistakable "Oooh, ooooh, unbelieeeevable, baby!" can be heard everywhere — during countless college games on ESPN and ABC, speaking engagements, endorsement appearances, interviews and his weekly radio show. Some critics accuse him of missing defensive subtleties but his exuberant telecasts are memorable — full of phrases like the "All-Bart Simpson Team" or "it's Maalox Time" — as he makes (and keeps) outrageous promises to his fans ("I'll stand on my head if X beats Y"). With one glass eye, this former college and NBA coach (Detroit Pistons) is one of the friendliest celebrities, spending $700 of his own money a month to mail fans basketballs, books and hats.

WALTON, BILL (Center, R, HF): This lanky, red-headed center is considered by many to be the best college player ever. He headed the "Walton Gang" under *John Wooden* at *UCLA* that amassed an 88-game win streak (still a record) and won 2 *NCAA* titles (1972 and 1973) as he was twice named *Final Four* MVP. In the NBA, his career with the Portland Trailblazers was cut short by knee problems, but not before he received the *Sixth Man Award* (1985-86), led the league in *blocked shots* (3.25 in 1976-77) and was named NBA *Finals* MVP 1976-77 while leading his team to the title. Knee problems in H.S. forced him to develop his *rebounding* to start the *fast-break* that marked his teams' successes. A cooperative, unselfish player, he is an intensely private, very outspoken man of convictions. His political involvements in anti-war campus demonstrations in May 1972 led to his arrest and the disapproval of his teammates. He also made the controversial decision not to represent the U.S. at the 1972 Munich Oympics where the U.S. lost the gold medal for the first time ever to Russia. Today he is a respected TV commentator and basketball analyst.

WEBBER, CHRIS (Center/Forward, A) His crucial error in calling a *timeout* his team did not have during the 1993 *NCAA* Final may have cost the Michigan Wolverines the title and will haunt him for years to come. Yet it was Webber's play that led the "Fab 5" to a 31-5 record and their 2nd consecutive trip to the NCAA finals, and he was applauded for the grace with which he handled an embarrassing situation. He was selected 1st overall in the *draft* after his sophomore year and offered the then-biggest NBA contract by the Golden State Warriors (15-year $74.4 million). As the league's youngest player, he led all rookies in *rebounding* (9.1 per game), *FG%* (.552) and *blocks* (164) on his way to becoming *Rookie of the Year* (1993-94) and an *All-Star*.

WEST, JERRY (Guard, R, HF): He joined the *L.A. Lakers* from West Virginia University for a career as one of the NBA's finest *guards*. Speed was his greatest asset and he got his graceful *jump shot* off faster and with more accuracy than anyone, as he averaged 27.0 *ppg* over his career (4th best all-time). Once he overcame his awe as a *rookie*, he unleashed a great *shooting touch* that was effective from anywhere on the floor. "Mr. Outside" made an explosive combination with *Elgin Baylor* on the *inside*. In 1969 he was NBA *Finals* MVP even though his team lost. It took 11 years before a 33-game winning streak (still a record) culminated in an NBA title (1972). That same year West led the league in *assists* and was voted MVP of the *All-Star Game*. Rumor has it that the NBA's logo of a basketball player is patterned after the left-handed West. He is currently the general manager of the Lakers.

WOODEN, JOHN (Coach, R, HF): This 3-time *All-American* (1930-32) was a brilliant scorer and defensive player at Purdue. As coach at Indiana State then *UCLA* (1949), he collected 664 wins, still 7th among all-time Division I coaches. By following the principles of his *Pyramid of Success* (See **Fig. 29**) he led a UCLA program with no facilities, no winning tradition and no recruiting to 10 *NCAA* titles (a record to this day, the next best is 4). His dream was to coach in the Big 10 so he stalled while awaiting an offer from Minnesota. When a snowstorm delayed the Minnesota offer an hour, he had accepted with UCLA and stuck to his word. The "Wizard of Westwood" originated the *full-court press* which revolutionized the game in the 1960s. He is the only individual to be twice-honored by the *Hall of Fame*. The 84-year old still sits in the corner bleachers of Pauley Pavilion during Bruin games, masking his emotions as carefully as ever.

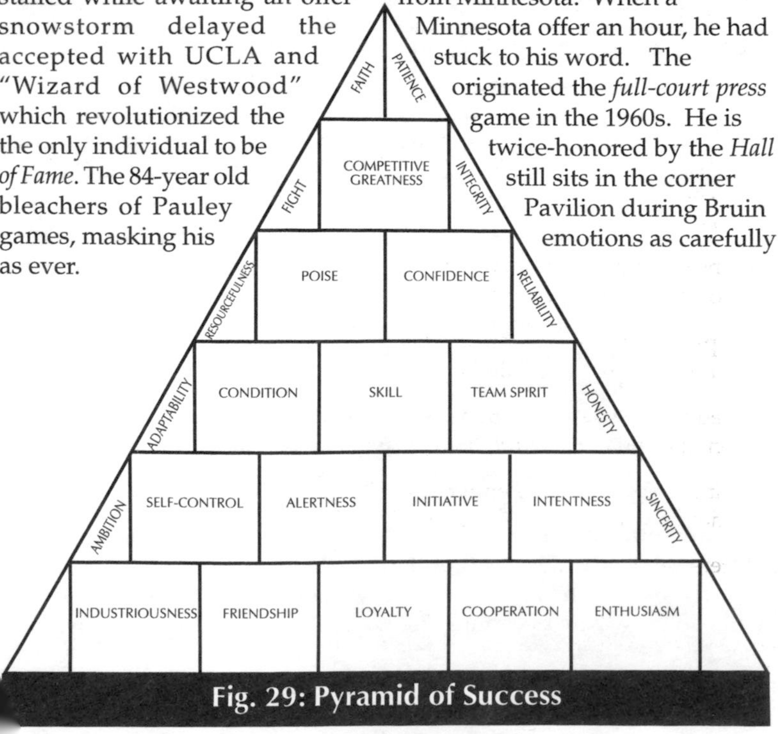

FAITH · PATIENCE

FIGHT · COMPETITIVE GREATNESS · INTEGRITY

RESOURCEFULNESS · POISE · CONFIDENCE · RELIABILITY

ADAPTABILITY · CONDITION · SKILL · TEAM SPIRIT · HONESTY

AMBITION · SELF-CONTROL · ALERTNESS · INITIATIVE · INTENTNESS · SINCERITY

INDUSTRIOUSNESS · FRIENDSHIP · LOYALTY · COOPERATION · ENTHUSIASM

Fig. 29: Pyramid of Success

GLOSSARY

alive: a ball is alive when it is released by a *shooter* or thrower, or legally tapped by a jumper during a *jump* ball; the *game clock* starts only when the ball becomes alive; compare with *live*.

alternating-possession rule: in college, the *possession arrow* changes direction after each subsequent *jump* ball situation, alternating which team gets *possession* for the *throw-in*.

assist: the last *pass* to a teammate that leads directly to a *field goal*; the scorer must move immediately toward the *basket* for the passer to be credited with an assist; only 1 assist can be credited per field goal.

backboard: the rectangular structure, 6' x 4', to which the *basket* is attached.

backcourt: the area from the *midcourt line* to the *end line* furthest from the *offense's basket*.

ball handler: the player with the ball; usually the *point guard* at the start of a play.

bank shot: a *shot* where the ball is first bounced (or banked) off the *backboard* at such an angle that it then drops into the *basket*.

baseline: see *end line*.

basket: attached to the *backboard*, it consists of a metal *rim* 18" in diameter suspended 10' from the *floor*, from which a 15-18" corded *net* hangs, and through which *points* are scored; also used to refer to a successful *field goal*.

beat the defender: when an offensive player, with or without the ball, is able to get past an opponent who is *guarding* him.

blind pass: a *pass* from a *ball handler* who does not see his *receiver*, but is estimating where he should be.

blocked shot: the successful deflection of a *shot* by touching part of the ball on its way to the *basket*, thereby preventing a *field goal*.

blocking: the use of a defender's body position to legally prevent an opponent's advance; the opposite of *charging*.

boosters: alumni supporters of college teams.

boxing out: a player's attempt to position his body between his opponents and the *basket* to get *rebounds* and prevent the opponents from doing so.

break: see *fast break*.

center circle: the circular area at *midcourt* from which *jump* balls are taken.

charging: an offensive *foul* which occurs when an offensive player runs into a defender who has *established position*.

clear out: see *one-on-one* showdown.

Commissioner: the president of the *NBA*.

court: the 94' x 50' area bounded by 2 *sidelines* and 2 *end lines* containing a *basket* at each end, on which a basketball game is played.

court vision: a player's ability to see everything on the *court* during play — such as where his teammates and defenders are set up — which enables him to make better choices in *passing*; the best *point guards* possess this.

crossover dribble: when a *ball handler dribbles* the ball across his body from one hand to the other.

cylinder: the imaginary area directly above the *basket* where *goaltending* or *basket interference* can occur.

dead ball: any ball that is not *live*; occurs after each successful *field goal* or *free-throw* attempt, after any *official's* whistle or if the ball leaves the *court*; it stops play which is then resumed by a *jump* ball, *throw-in* or *free-throw*.

defense: the act of preventing the *offense* from scoring; the team without the ball.

defensive rebound: a *rebound* by a player on *defense*.

double team: when two teammates join efforts in *guarding* a single opponent.

downcourt or down the court: the direction a team on *offense* moves, from its *backcourt* into its *frontcourt* and towards its own *basket*.

draft: the method by which *NBA* teams annually select college or *foreign players* to their teams, designed to promote balanced competition in the NBA.

Dream Team: the name given by the media to the U.S. basketball team that won the gold medal at the 1992 Barcelona Olympics; it was the first time non-amateurs were permitted to represent the country; the members of this team were *Charles Barkley, Larry Bird,* Clyde Drexler, *Patrick Ewing, Magic Johnson, Michael Jordan,* Christian Laettner, Karl Malone, Chris Mullin, Scottie Pippen, *David Robinson* and *John Stockton*.

Dream Team II: the name given by the media to the U.S. team that won the 1994 *FIBA World Cup* in Toronto, Canada; its members were *Derrick Coleman*, Joe Dumars, Tim Hardaway, *Larry Johnson*, Kevin Johnson, Shawn Kemp, Dan Majerle, Reggie Miller, Alonzo Mourning, *Shaquille O'Neal*, Mark Price, Steve Smith, Isiah Thomas and Dominique Wilkins.

dribble or dribbling: when a player repeatedly pushes, pats, taps or bats the ball toward the *floor* with one hand to cause the ball to bounce back up to either of his hands; used to advance the ball or keep control of it.

dribble series: a number of consecutive *dribbles* which end when a player allows the ball to rest in one or both hands; a player is only permitted one dribble series before he must *pass* or *shoot*.

drive to the basket: to move rapidly toward the *basket* with the ball.

dunk: when a player close to the *basket* jumps and strongly throws the ball down into it; an athletic, creative *shot* used to intimidate opponents.

elbowing: it is a *violation* if a player vigorously or excessively swings his elbows, even if there is no contact; it is a *foul* if contact is made, and an automatic ejection if that contact is above shoulder level.

end line: the boundary line behind each *basket*; also called the *baseline*.

established position: when a defensive player has both feet firmly planted on the *floor* before an offensive player's head and shoulder get past him; the offensive player who runs into such a defender is *charging*.

fake or feint: a deceptive move to throw a defender off balance and allow an offensive player to *shoot* or receive a *pass*; players use their eyes, head or any other part of the body to trick an opponent.

fast break: also called the run-and-shoot offense, it begins with a *defensive rebound* by a player who immediately sends an *outlet pass* toward *midcourt* to his waiting teammates; these teammates can sprint to their *basket* and quickly *shoot* before enough opponents catch up to stop them.

field goal: when the ball enters the *basket* from above during play; worth 2 *points*, or 3 points if the *shooter* was standing behind the *3-point line*.

Finals, NBA: the annual championship series of the *NBA*'s *post-season*.

Final Four: the 4 regional champions (West, East, Midwest and Southeast) remaining from the 64 college teams that compete in the annual *NCAA Tournament*; they play one another to determine the national champion.

flagrant foul: unnecessary or excessive contact against an opponent.

floor: the area of the *court* within the *end lines* and *sidelines*.

floor violation: a player's action that violates the rules but does not prevent an opponent's movement or cause him harm; penalized by a change in *possession*.

forwards: the 2 players on the *court* for a team who are usually smaller than the *center* and bigger than the *guards*; often a team's highest scorers.

foul: actions by players which break the rules but are not *floor violations*; penalized by a change in *possession* or *free-throw* opportunities; see *personal foul* or *technical foul*.

foul lane: the painted area 19' x 16' (12' in college) bordered by the *end line* and the *foul line*, outside which players must stand during a *free-throw*; also the area an offensive player cannot spend more than 3-*seconds* at a time in.

foul line: the line 15' from the *backboard* and parallel to the *end line* from which players shoot *free-throws*.

foul shot: see *free-throw*.

4-point play: a *3-point shot* followed by a successful *free-throw*.

franchise: a professional team.

franchise player: a star player around which a *franchise* is built.

free agent, restricted: an *NBA* player whose contract has expired and who may negotiate with any team, but his original team retains the right of first refusal to make an offer at least 125% of the player's previous salary or $250,000 (whichever is greater) within 15 days of another team making an offer.

free agent, unrestricted: an *NBA free agent* who is not subject to the right of first refusal (see *free agent, restricted*); he must have completed at least his 2nd contract and have more than 5 years in the NBA, or he must have been terminated ("put on waivers") by his team.

free-throw: an un*guard*ed shot taken from the *foul line* by a player whose opponent committed a *personal* or *technical foul*; it is worth 1 *point*.

free-throw line: see *foul line*.

free-throw line extended: an imaginary line drawn from the *free-throw* line to the *sideline* to determine the location for certain *throw-ins*.

frontcourt: the area between the *midcourt line* and the *end line* closest to the *offense*'s *basket*.

full-court press: when defenders start *guarding* the *offense* in the *backcourt*.

game clock: shows how much time remains in each of the four 12-minute *quarters* of an *NBA* game or two 20-minute *halves* of a college game.

guards: the 2 players on each team who are the smallest on the *court*; they usually handle setting up plays and *passing* to teammates closer to the *basket*.

guarding: the act of following an opponent around the *court* to prevent him from getting close to the *basket*, taking an *open shot* or making easy an *pass*, while avoiding illegal contact.

half-court or *set offense*: when a team takes the time to develop a play in its *frontcourt*, such as the *give-and-go* or a *screening play*; opposite of *fast break*.

high percentage shot: a *shot* that is likely to go in the *basket*, such as a *layup*.

high post: an imaginary area outside either side of the *foul lane* at the *free-throw line extended*.

in the paint: being in the *foul lane* area which is painted a different color.

inbounds: the area within the *end lines* and *sidelines* of the *court*; also the act of bringing the ball into this area by means of a *throw-in*.

incidental contact: minor contact usually overlooked by *officials*.

inside shooting: *shots* taken by a player near or under the *basket*.

jump ball: 2 opposing players jump for a ball an *official* tosses above and between them, to tap it to their teammates and gain *possession*; used to start the game (*tip-off*) and all *overtime periods*, and sometimes to *restart* play.

keepaway game: a tactic used by the team that is leading near the end of a *period* to keep the ball from its opponents to prevent them from scoring while using up time off the *game clock*; also called *freezing*.

key or keyhole: the area at each end of the *court* consisting of the *foul circle*, *foul lane* and *free-throw line*; named for the shape it had years ago.

layup or layin: a shot taken after *driving to the basket* by leaping up under the *basket* and using one hand to drop the ball directly into the basket (layin) or to *bank* the ball off the *backboard* into it (layup).

leading the receiver: when a *passer* throws the ball where he thinks a *receiver* is headed.

live ball: as soon as a ball is given to a *free-throw shooter* or a *thrower* on a *throw-in*, it is live, but the *game clock* does not restart until the ball is *alive*.

loose ball: a ball that is *alive* but not in the *possession* of either team.

low post: an imaginary area outside either side of the *foul lane* close to the *basket*.

lower percentage shot: a *shot* that is less likely to go in the *basket*, such as one thrown by a player who is off balance or outside his *shooting range*.

man-to-man defense: the defensive style used in the NBA, where each defensive player is responsible for *guarding* one opponent.

March Madness: see *NCAA Tournament*.

match-ups: any pairing of players on opposing teams who *guard* each other.

MVP (Most Valuable Player): an award recognizing the *NBA* player who contributed most to the *regular season* or to the *Finals*.

NBA (National Basketball Association): a professional league created in 1949 that now has 27 teams in the U.S. and is adding 2 Canadian teams in 1995.

NCAA (National Collegiate Athletic Association): a voluntary association of over 1,000 colleges and universities in the U.S. whose role is to establish standards and protect the integrity of amateurism for student-athletes.

NCAA Tournament: an annual competition between 64 college teams to crown a national champion; also called *March Madness* because the three-week-long event is held during March; see also *Final Four*.

NIT (National Invitational Tournament): the oldest college tournament, in which 32 teams not selected to the *NCAA Tournament* compete each year.

off the dribble: a *shot* taken while *driving to the basket*.

offense: the team with *possession* of the ball.

offensive rebound: a *rebound* by a player on offense.

officials: the *crew chief*, *referee* and *umpire* who control the game, stop and start play, and impose penalties for *violations* and *fouls*.

1-and-1 or 1-plus-1: in college, a *free-throw* attempt awarded for certain *violations* that earns the *shooter* a 2nd attempt only <u>if</u> the first is successful.

open: when a player is un*guard*ed by a defender.

out of bounds: the area outside of and including the *end lines* and *sidelines*.

outside shooting: *shots* taken from the *perimeter*.

over the limit: when a team commits more than 5 *team fouls* per *NBA period* (4 in each *overtime*) or more than 7 per *half* in college.

overtime or OT: the extra *period*(s) played after a *regulation game* ends *tied*.

pass: when a *passer* throws the ball to a teammate; used to *start* plays, move the ball *downcourt*, keep it away from defenders and get it to a *shooter*.

passer: the player who *passes* the ball to a teammate.

period: any *quarter*, *half* or *overtime* segment.

perimeter: the area beyond the *foul circle* away from the *basket*, including *3-point line*, from which players take long-range shots.

personal foul: contact between players that may result in *injury* or provide one team with an unfair advantage; players may not *push*, *hold*, trip, hack, *elbow*, restrain or *charge* into an opponent; these are also counted as *team fouls*.

picked off: refers to a defender who has been successfully prevented from reaching the *ball handler* by an offensive *screen*.

pick-up games: impromptu games played among players who just met.

pivot: a *center*; also the foot that must remain touching the *floor* until a *ball handler* who has stopped *dribbling* is ready to *pass* or *shoot*.

playmaker: the *point guard* who generally sets up plays for his teammates.

point-shaving: an illegal practice where players intentionally win a game, but by fewer *points* than the *point spread*; led to 2 major college scandals (involved 32 of the biggest stars in the 1950s, then 22 colleges in 1961).

point spread: a device established by bookmakers to equalize 2 teams for betting purposes; e.g., if a team is considered to be 4 points better than another, the spread is 4 points; to win a bet on the favorite, that team would need to win by more than the spread (in this case, by more than 4 points); the margin of victory is more important than whether a team wins or loses.

possession: to be holding or in control of the ball.

possession arrow: in college, used to determine which team's turn it is to *inbounds* the ball to begin a *period* or in a *jump ball* situation.

post position: the position of a player standing in the *low post* or *high post*.

quadruple double: a *triple double* with double-digits scored in 4 categories.

rebound: when a player grabs a ball that is coming off the *rim* or *backboard* after a *shot* attempt; see *offensive rebound* and *defensive rebound*.

receiver: the player who receives a *pass* from the *ball handler*.

regulation game: four 12-minute *quarters* in the NBA or two 20-minute *halves* in college; a game that ends without *overtime periods*.

release: the moment that the ball leaves a *shooter's* hands.

rookie: a player in his first NBA season.

roster: the list of players on a team.

run: occurs when one team scores several *field goals* in quick succession while its opponents score few or none.

salary cap: an annual dollar limit that a single team may pay all its players.

scoring opportunity: when a player gets *open* for a *shot* that is likely to score.

screen or screener: the offensive player who stands between a teammate and a defender to gives his teammate the chance to take an *open shot*.

shot clock: a clock that limits the time a team with the ball has to shoot it; *24 seconds* in the NBA; in college, *35 seconds* for men, *30 seconds* for women.

shooter: a player who takes a *shot* at the *basket*.

shooter's roll: the ability to get even an inaccurate *shot* to bounce lightly off the *rim* and into the *basket*

shooting range: the distance from which a player is likely to make his *shots*.

sidelines: 2 boundary lines that run the length of the *court*.

sixth man: the best *substitute* on a team; usually the first player to come off the *bench* to replace a *starter*.

slam dunk: see *dunk*.

squaring up: when a player's shoulders are facing the *basket* as he *releases* the ball for a *shot*; considered good shooting position.

starting lineup: the 5 *starters* who begin a game; usually a team's best players.

substitute: a player who comes into the game to replace a player on the *court*.

swing man: a player who can play both the *guard* and *forward* positions.

team fouls: each *personal foul* committed by a player is also counted against his team; when a team goes *over the limit*, its opponent is awarded *free-throw* opportunities.

technical fouls or Ts: procedural violations and misconduct that *officials* believe are detrimental to the game; penalized by a single *free-throw* opportunity to the non-offending team (2 free-throws in college).

3-on-3: a game played with only 3 players on the *court* for each team.

3-point play: a 2-point *field goal* followed by a successful *free-throw*.

3-point shot: a *field goal* worth 3 points because the *shooter* had both feet on the *floor* behind the *3-point line* when he *released* the ball; also counts if one foot is behind the line while the other is in the air.

throw-in: the method by which a team with *possession inbounds* the ball.

timeout: when play is temporarily suspended by an *official* or at the request of a team to discuss strategy or respond to an injured player; there are *full timeouts* (100 seconds in the *NBA*, 75 seconds in college) and *20-second timeouts*.

tip-off: the initial *jump* ball that starts the game.

transition: the shift from *offense* to *defense*.

traveling: a *floor violation* when the *ball handler* takes too many steps without dribbling; also called *walking*.

triple double: when a player scores double-digits in 3 categories during one game (*points, assists* and *rebounds* are most common, but it can also be *blocks* or *steals*); a sign of great versatility.

turnover: when the *offense* loses *possession* through its own fault by passing the ball *out of bounds* or committing a *floor violation*.

upset: when a higher-*seeded* (better) team beats a lower-seeded (inferior) one.

violation: see *floor violation*.

weakside: the side of the *court* away from the ball.

zone defense: a defense used extensively in college but not permitted in the *NBA*, where each *defender* is responsible for an area of the *court* and must *guard* any player who enters that area.

INDEX

Bolded page numbers indicate a photograph, diagram or table.

leading the receiver 26, 117
live ball 19, 53, 117
lob pass 28
loose ball 15, 18, 46, 53, 118, **127**
Los Angeles Lakers 71, 93, 95, 96, 98, 102, 104, 112
lottery 77-78
low post **7**, 32, **39**, 61, 118, 119

M

Malone, Moses 89, 90, 95, 106
man-to-man defense 64, 65, 118
Maravich, Pete 91, 106
March Madness 82, 118
match-ups 58, 118
midcourt line **7**, 9, 22, 46, 47
Midwest Division 68, **71**
Mikan, George 106-107
mismatch 18, 58
Most Valuable Player, See *MVP*
MVP 95, 96, 118

N

Naismith, Dr. James **1**, 4, 5, 94
National Basketball Association, See *NBA*
National Basketball League, See *NBL*
National Collegiate Athletic Association, See *NCAA*
National Invitational Tournament, See *NIT*
NBA ii, 4, 67-**71**, 72-75, 77-79, 80, 89, 92, 95, 118
NBA Finals 72-**74**, 92, 96, 115
NBA playoffs 72-73, **74**
NBA teams 68-**71**, 92
NBL (National Basketball League) ii, 4, 68
NCAA ii, 3, 4, 50, 77, 80-**83**, 84, 93, 115, 118
NCAA Tournament 81-82, **83**, 115, 118
net **8**, **9**, 113
NIT 84, 93, 118
non-shooting foul **44**, 45, 51

O

offense 15, 34, 58, 59-63, 118
offensive rebound 34, 86, 87, 90, 118
official game clock, See *clock, game*
officials 18, 24, 41-42, 99, 118
officials' hand signals **122-125**
Olajuwon, Hakeem 103, 107
on the line 66
1-plus-1 *or* 1-and-1 45, 51, 118
one-on-one 11, 14, 61, 64, 114
O'Neal, Shaquille 107, 115
open 26, 29, 58, 59, 118
OR, See *rebound, offensive*
Original Celtics 3, 92, 94
OT, See *overtime*
out of bounds **6**, 10, 15, 18, 46, 86, 118, 129
outlet pass 27, 62, 115
outside shooting 12, 38, 112, 119
over the limit **44**, 45, 51, 119, 121
overhead pass **28**
overtime 14, 23, 117, 119, 120

P

Pacific Division 68, **71**
paint, in the, See *foul lane*
palming 43, 47
Parish, Robert 98, 101
passes, types of 27-29
passing 15, 26-29, 48, 67, 119
perimeter 12, 27, 38, 39, 61, 65, 67, 109, 119
period 14, 21, 119
personal foul 18, 19, 21, 41, 43, 50-53, 56, 116, 119, 121, **127**
pick, See *screen*
pick-and-roll 60
pick-up game 37, 106, 119
pinch-post 59
Player of the Year, (college) 97, 108, 109
Player of the Year, NBA, See *MVP*
playmaker, See *point guard*
player-control foul 53
Players' Association 79
playoffs, NBA, See *NBA playoffs*
Podoloff, Maurice 75, 95
point guard 38, 98, 104, 105, 110, 113, 114, 119
point-shaving 93, 109, 119
points-per-game 85
possession 6, 15, 16-18, 20, 21-22, 43, 46, 49, 53, 54, 56, 66, 67, 86, 119
possession arrow 18, 54, 113, 119
post, high, See *high post*
post, low, See *low post*
post-season 72, 95, 115
PPG, See *points-per-game*
posting up 39, 109
public address operator 14
punched ball 47
pushing 53, **129**
Pyramid of Success **112**

Q

quadruple double 107, 109, 120
quarters 14, 16, 119

R

rebound, defensive 34, 62, 86, 114
rebound, offensive 34, 62, 86, 118
rebounds 34, 86, 90, 100, 103, 105, 107, 108, 109, 113
rebounds, total 86
receiver 26, 28, 59, 113, 117, 120
record 72, 74, 75, 81, 92, 93
records, college *and* NBA **89-91**
referee 41, 94, 110, 118
Regional Finals 82
regular season 72, 97
regulation 14, 23, 120
release 13, 30, 31, 32, 48, 120
Rens, N.Y. 3, 92, 94
restarting play 19
Riley, Patrick 93, 95, 108
rim 8, 11, 19, 21, 33, 46, 47, 48, 49
Robertson, Oscar 89, 90, 95, 108

Robinson, David 89, 96, 108-109, 114
Robinson, Glenn 109
rookie 76
Rookie of the Year 95, 98, 100, 101, 102, 103, 104, 107, 108, 111
roster 37, 75, 77, 120
round 72-73, 77, 82, 83, 84
run 13, 120
run-and-shoot offense, See *fast break*
Rupp, Adolph 97, 109
Russell, Bill 90, 95, 99, 102, 109

S

salary cap 79, 107, 110, 120
Schick Award 96, 99, 108
scorers 10, 41-42
scorers' table 7, 10, 42
scoring average 85
scoring opportunity 33, 38, 120
screen 3, 34, 49, 59-**60**, 120
screen-and-roll, See *pick-and-roll*
screen, double 61
screen, illegal 49, 53, **129**
screening plays 59-60
seeded 73-**74**, 82, **83**, 84
set offense, See *half-court offense*
set shot 31
shooting 30-33, 38, **44**, 45-46
shooting guard 38
shot blocking, See *blocked shots*
shot clock **8**, 21-22, 30, 42, 49, 67, 120
shot selection 30
shot, types of 30-33
sidearm pass 28
sideline 6, **7**, 120
sixth man 96, 111, 120
skyhook 33, 98
slam dunk, See *dunk*
splitting **60**-61
stack 61
standings **88**
starting lineup 25, 37, 42, 55, 86, 120
stopping play 19
starting play 19
steals 15, 36, 86, 87, 91
Stern, David 110
Stockton, John 90, 105, 110, 114
Strom, Earl 110
substitutes 25, 37, 40, 42, 51, 58, 66, 121
substitution box **7**, 10, 25
swing man 38, 121

T

Ts, See *technical foul*
tap pass 16, 28
target area **8**
Tarkanian, Jerry 109, 110
team fouls 42, 43, **44**, 45, 50-51, 119, 121
team standings **87**
technical foul 12, 21, 24, **44**, 46, 48, 52, 54-56, 121, **127**
technicals, double 54
television replay 42

10-second violation 22, 47-48, 64, 66
thread-the-needle pass 28
3-on-3 14, 121
3-point field goal percentage 85
3-point line **7**, 10, 12, 46, 54, 66, 115, 119, 121
3-point shot 65, 90, **127**
3-point play 12, 45, 121
3-seconds violation 48, **128**
30-second clock 21; See also *shot clock*
35-second clock 21; See also *shot clock*
35-second violation 21, 49
throw-in 18, 19, **20**, 22, 43, **44**, 45, 48, 66, 121
throw-in locations **44**
throw-in violation 48
timers *or* timekeepers 10, 41, 42
timeout, commercial 23
timeout, full 23, 121, **126**
timeout, mandatory 23
timeout, official's 21, 24
timeout, 20-second 23, 121, **126**
timeout watch 42
tip in 33, 40
tip-off 16, **17**, 18, 117, 121
touch pass 28
TR, See *rebounds, total*
trading deadline 79
transition 39, 61, 62, 64, 121
traveling 31, 34, 48, 121, **128**
triple double 101, 104
turnaround 36
turnovers 13, 15, 16, 35, 63, 110, 121
24-second clock 21, 22, 56, 107; See also *shot clock*
24-second violation 21, 49, **128**

U

UCLA 93, 98, 111, 112
umpire 41, 118
uniforms 11
upset 84, 99, 121

V

violation, See *floor violation*
Vitale, Dick 111

W

walking, See *traveling*
Walton, Bill 97, 111
weakside 47, 61, 121
Webb, Spud 98
Webber, Chris 24, 111
West, Jerry 89, 96, 112
Western Conference 68, **71**
win-loss record 72, 77, 110
wing lanes 58
winning percentage 72, 93, 108, 109, 110
women's basketball 4, 21, 81
Wooden, John 93, 94, 97, 98, 109, 111, 112
World Cup ii, 102, 115

Z

zone defense 55, 64-**65**, 121

OFFICIALS' HAND SIGNALS

TIME IN: chopping motion with a hand or finger.

TIMEOUT or **STOP CLOCK**: arm raised with open palm facing out. (See p. 23)

20-SECOND TIME-OUT: both hands touching shoulders. (See p. 23)

DIRECTION OF PLAY: arm outstretched in front of the body with a finger pointing in the direction while the color of the team going on offense is called.

JUMP BALL: thumbs of both hands raised above the head. (See p. 16)

CANCEL SCORE, CANCEL PLAY or **NO SCORE**: outstretched arms crossed then uncrossed in front of the body.

3-POINT FIELD GOAL: one arm is raised above the head when an attempt is made, and the other is raised if the shot is successful. (See p. 12)

PERSONAL FOUL: clenched fist raised above the head. (See p. 50)

DOUBLE FOUL: clenched fists waved across each other above the head. (See p. 56)

TECHNICAL FOUL: both hands used to form the letter "T" at chest level. (See p. 54)

LOOSE BALL FOUL: both arms extended to the side at shoulder level. (See p. 53)

TO DESIGNATE AN OFFENDER: fingers held up to indicate the player's jersey number (each hand represents one digit). (See p. 41)

BASKET INTERFERENCE: finger of one hand rotated around a fist formed by the other hand in front of the body. (See p. 50)

GOALTENDING: 2 fingers waved downward to indicate 2 points are being awarded to the offense. (See p. 49)

3-SECOND RULE INFRACTION: 3 fingers held up in the air. (See p. 48)

TRAVELING: two clenched fists and forearms rotated around each other in front of the body. (See p. 48)

24-SECOND VIOLATION: top of the head tapped with an open palm. (See p. 49)

BLOCKING: both hands placed on the hips. (See p. 52)

CHARGING: clenched fist with the arm outstretched to the side at shoulder level. (See p. 52)

HOLDING: one wrist grabbed with the opposite hand. (See p. 53)

ILLEGAL DEFENSE: one arm folded at chest level extended parallel to the floor. (See p. 55)

ILLEGAL DRIBBLE or **DOUBLE DRIBBLE**: patting motion in front of the body with one hand at a time. (See p. 46)

ILLEGAL SCREEN OUT OF BOUNDS: arms crossed at chest level. (See p.49)

ILLEGAL USE OF HANDS: forearm area struck with the pinky side of the opposite hand.

ISOLATION: both arms outstretched and brought down from the shoulder to the waist. (See p. 47)

PUSHING: pushing motion with both palms facing out from the chest. (See p. 53)

ORDER FORM

Order any of the following Spectator Guides:

Title	Qty	Price	Total
Basketball Made Simple		$7.95	
Football Made Simple		$7.95	
Ice Hockey Made Simple		$7.95	
Soccer Made Simple		$7.95	
		Subtotal	
Add $2.00 per book for shipping & handling		S&H	
		Sales Tax (CA)	
		Total	

Order by phone toll-free: **800-247-8228**

or send form to : First Base Sports, Inc.
P.O. Box 1731
Manhattan Beach, CA 90267-1731

Name _____

Street Address _____

City _____

State _____ Zip _____

Phone No. _____

<u>Method of Payment</u>:

Check ❏ or Charge: VISA ❏ Master Card ❏

Card # _____ Exp. Date (required) _____

Signature _____ B/94